PEOPLES OF ROMAN BRITAIN

General Editor Keith Branigan
Lecturer in Archaeology in the University of Bristol

THE
CORITANI

MALCOLM TODD

Lecturer in Archaeology in the University of Nottingham

DUCKWORTH

First published in 1973 by
Gerald Duckworth and Co. Ltd.
The Old Piano Factory,
43 Gloucester Crescent,
London, NW1

© Malcolm Todd 1973

Cloth ISBN 0 7156 0649 2

Paper ISBN 0 7156 0698 0

CC

711383

6000274497

Typeset in Great Britain by
Specialised Offset Services Ltd., Liverpool,
and printed by
Unwin Brothers Ltd., Old Woking, Surrey.

For my wife

Acknowledgments

Many people have helped me to produce this book, some during the writing of it, many more during the collection of material. First of all I must thank the many workers in the field of Roman Britain whose results (whether published or not) I am here setting forth. Their names cannot be listed for they are legion. Particular debts were incurred during composition. I would like especially to thank Mr A.D. MacWhirr for his help over the Roman period settlements in Leicestershire and for discussion of many wider problems. Mr A.L.F. Rivet and Dr G. Webster kindly read and improved early drafts of individual chapters. Further contributions, in the form of photographs, have been made by Mrs G.R.C. Harding, Mr D.N. Riley, Dr J.K. St. Joseph and by Leicester and Lincoln Museums.

Preface

Even the most superficial acquaintance with the archaeology of the Roman Empire will make it plain that those who work in this field are studying not one single organism but an enormous complex of local cultures, to a greater or lesser degree disguised by a facade of Roman civilisation. Study of these local cultures, particularly in the western provinces, is severely limited by the fact that the prime source for them is archaeology. For numerous aspects of their history, indeed, it is the only source. No book which, like this one, is based primarily on archaeological evidence will ever be a complete survey of its field. Almost every subject studied here requires more discussion that I have had space for. *Malheur aux détails, c'est une vermine qui tue les grands ouvrages.* I have often had cause to agree with Voltaire and this *ouvrage* has more than its fair share of *détails*. Compression will be most obvious in the chapters which deal with rural settlement and the industries. With reluctance some subjects have been omitted entirely. One of these is the matter of field-systems, and this can only be justified by the fact that the peculiar difficulties of the subject need more than a few paragraphs for their adumbration. There are other problems which will one day require discussion. One of the most important is the relationship between the *territoria* of Lincoln and Leicester. It must be borne in mind that the division of the tribal land of the Coritani between the cities of *Lindum* and *Ratae* may have had a profound influence upon the development of land-settlement in particular. The Roman colony of Lincoln itself, of course, must be excluded from this account, but what is to be done about its territory? Since as yet no clear distinction can be drawn between the territories of the two cities, I have dealt with the area up to the walls of Lincoln as though it formed part of the *civitas Coritanorum*. The reader will bear in mind that it did not, and that this proceeding can strictly be justified only on the grounds that the limits of the territory of Lincoln cannot be drawn with any confidence. Another area has been deliberately omitted. This is the Fenland of south Lincolnshire, most probably administered as part of an Imperial estate by agents of the Emperor and not as tribal land by the *ordo* at Leicester. In any case, for the time being the reader can do no better than refer to the monograph produced by the Royal Geographical Society (Phillips *1970*).

In dealing with one of the tribes of Roman Britain, the writer must at an early time declare what he believes its boundaries were. In the case of the Coritani, as of the other Romano-British tribes, these are given to us by no ancient source. Ultimately we are compelled to adopt limits for the tribes on the basis of an amalgam of reason, guesswork and convenience. The suggested boundaries for the Coritani will, I trust, prove generally acceptable. That they cannot be put forward as the proven limits will be obvious to anyone with the merest acquaintance with Romano-British documentary sources.

Although one of the largest of the Romano-British tribes, the Coritani have no *persona*. No Cunobelin or Boudicca has given them an identity. Lying between the Brigantes and the Catuvellauni, they make a poor showing in the scanty ancient sources on Roman Britain and they are no more prominent in modern works on the province. Nevertheless they occupied one of the most fertile regions of Britain and their land nourished two of the more important of Romano-British cities, *Lindum Colonia* and *Ratae Coritanorum*. The effort to understand what the Coritani made of their territory under Roman rule may be strenuous and at many points doomed to frustration. From year to year, however, the archaeological evidence is growing. A framework is now sorely needed within which this evidence can be properly interpreted, and this I have attemped to provide.

M.T.

Contents

List of Illustrations

Line Drawings by Jennifer Gill

1.

Tribal territory and the pre-Roman Iron Age

In the past twelve years our knowledge of the settlements and material culture of the Iron Age inhabitants of Coritanian territory has been greatly enlarged. Down to about 1960, few Iron Age settlements of the period immediately preceding the Roman invasion had been identified, much less excavated. This state of affairs is now being rectified but our information leaves much to be desired. It is still far from possible to give a full account of the Coritani in the Iron Age, but since their descendants formed the Roman *civitas*, their cultural background is a proper field of study for the student of this, as of any other, part of the western Roman provinces. Fresh information about the Iron Age tribe will ultimately mean new light on the Roman *civitas*.

The east Midlands were for long believed to have lain outside the range of effective cultural influence from the Belgic peoples of south-east England headed by the Catuvellauni. The material culture of the Catuvellaunian confederacy, Iron Age C, was held to extend no further north than the valley of the Nene. Occasional finds of Iron Age C pottery and metalwork in the east Midlands were interpreted as trade-objects. The Coritani were not recognised as having any well defined cultural characteristics (archaeological material of the half century on either side of the birth of Christ being scarce) and were therefore generally assumed to be a rather insignificant people, less advanced than their thrusting southern neighbours and less dynamic than the Brigantes of the Pennines. The latter were even thought to be one cultural stage ahead of the Coritani in that they had

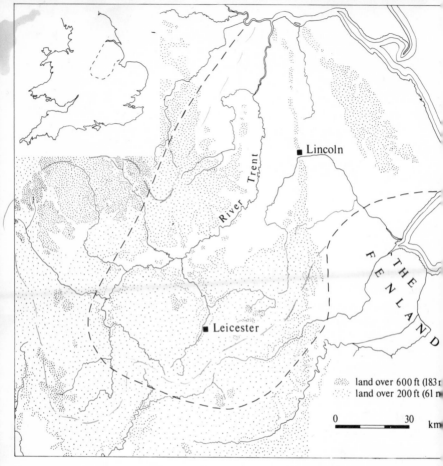

land over 600 ft (183 m)
land over 200 ft (61 m)

0   30
         km

1. The extent of the *civitas Coritanorum*

apparently adopted a system of Belgic-style coinage, deriving
it from the currency of the south-eastern dynasts, whereas
the Coritani seemed to have minted no coins of their own.
D. F. Allen's work on the Iron Age coinages of Britain[1] has
radically altered the picture. The coins formerly attributed to
the Brigantes can now be assigned to the Coritani on the
evidence of their distribution, which includes Lincolnshire,
Leicestershire and Rutland with a few outliers west of the
Trent. In the Brigantian area proper, the coins would appear
extremely rare but for two hoards found at Lightcliffe and
Honley in the valley of the Calder,[2] and it is clear that they
did not normally circulate as far north as this. The Lightcliffe

and Honley hoards, which have so long clouded the tribal origin of these coins, are probably to be interpreted as merchants' hoards or perhaps as the hastily concealed riches of wealthy Coritanian refugees fleeing the advance of Rome.

Much more significant than the attribution of a Belgic-style coinage to the Coritani is the fact that excavation of a number of Iron Age settlements has begun to yield pottery and metalwork which is closely related to that from Iron Age C settlements and cemeteries in south-eastern England (fig. 2). Hardly any of the excavations which have brought this material to light have yet been published and thus only the baldest summary of current opinion is possible.

Excavations at the Jewry Wall site in the centre of Leicester from 1936 to 1939[3] produced an early indication of an Iron Age C strain among the Coritani. Here, Dr Kathleen Kenyon found pottery and a few bronze objects whose character suggested that the Leicester site may have been occupied before the Roman invasion by a people whose culture was akin to Iron Age C. The precise significance of this material from the earliest levels at Jewry Wall has never been agreed on, for none of it can be dated closely. Much, if not all, of Dr Kenyon's material could have been carried to Leicester *after* A.D. 43 by a Roman military unit and those associated with it. In the nineteen-sixties, however, Iron Age C pottery which certainly dates from well before 43 has been found here,[4] thus demonstrating finally that the Roman city of *Ratae*, like several other tribal centres in southern Britain, had had a pre-Roman ancestor. Presumably the Iron Age site at Leicester was a principal centre of the Coritani. The pottery in question, all of it recovered during rescue excavation within the Roman walled circuit, includes pedestal urns and cordoned bowls which have close relatives in the Aylesford-Swarling cultural assemblage. Its date is probably to be set within the first four decades of the first century A.D. Two further sites, Ancaster and Old Sleaford[5] (both in central Lincolnshire), have recently produced large quantities of Iron Age C pottery (fig. 3) and numbers of Coritanian coins. Old Sleaford, moreover, was the site of an Iron Age mint, as is revealed by some 3,000 fragments of the clay moulds in which coin-flans were cast. For a time at least,

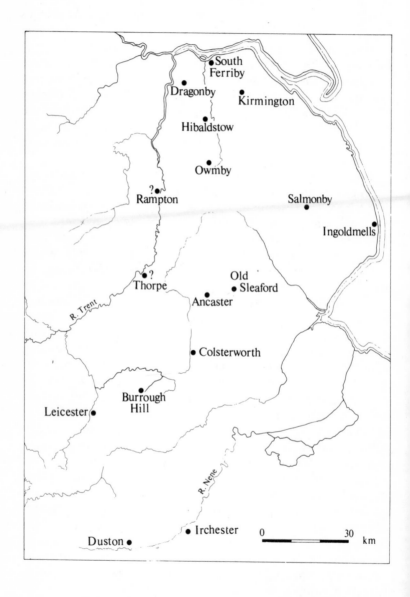

2. Iron Age C material in the north-east Midlands

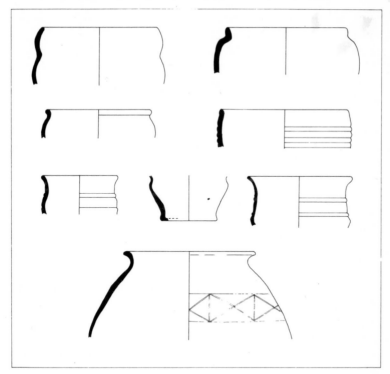

3. Iron Age C pottery from Ancaster (Lincs.)

then, this was the residence of either a tribal or a local ruler. The extent of both Iron Age Ancaster and Old Sleaford makes it clear that they were major settlements, although in neither case is there any trace of the kind of defences provided for Iron Age *oppida* further south.

More informative and cogent still is the evidence from the extensive excavation of a large settlement at Dragonby, near Scunthorpe.[6] This site lies close to the Jurassic Way and some six miles from the confluence of the Trent with the Humber. Here an Iron Age B occupation of the late second and early first century B.C. was gradually transformed into an Iron Age C assemblage during the succeeding century. By the early years of the first century A.D. and quite possibly by the later decades of the first century B.C., similarities in vessel-forms and in their fabrics are detectable between the Dragonby pottery and that from Camulodunum and other Catuvel-launian centres. There is, however, no hint of drastic cultural realignment, no sudden intrusion from outside. The process of change seems ever gradual and, throughout the period of transformation, native elements continued to assert them-selves. Thus the contribution of Dragonby is to clinch the case for a strong cultural association between the Coritani and the Belgic peoples of the south-east, while stressing the continued working of 'native' or east Midland traditions in the making of pottery.

North Lincolnshire has several other large sites which have produced quantities of Iron Age C occupation material: e.g. Kirmington, South Ferriby and Owmby.[7] Several hoards of Iron Age coins from the south shore of the Humber, at South Ferriby and Grimsby[8] in particular, point to the activity of merchants using the Humber crossings, and incidentally hint at the prosperity of Coritanian chiefs. Agriculture will hardly account for this. A much more likely source of wealth in a society geared to war is iron, in which north-west Lincoln-shire abounds.[9]

Several minor settlements have also revealed strong links with the south-east in material culture. The most completely examined so far is that at Colsterworth in south Lincoln-shire[10] (fig. 4). Here a group of huts, including one rather larger than the four or five others, was found to lie within an irregular ditched enclosure of a little over one acre in size. This little village, probably the steading of one family and its adherents, was occupied about the time of the Roman conquest and perhaps a little later. It is one of several Iron Age settlements in an area rich in surface deposits of iron-stone. Further traces of Iron Age C pottery come from the Lincolnshire coast, notably from Ingoldmells and Skeg-ness, where its association is with salt-making by the evaporation of brine.[11]

As yet, the evidence for Iron Age C culture in the region is strongest in Lincolnshire. In the other parts of the tribal territory the picture is by no means so clear. Very few sites in the Trent valley have yet been examined, but such indica-tions as there are suggest that Iron Age C culture was

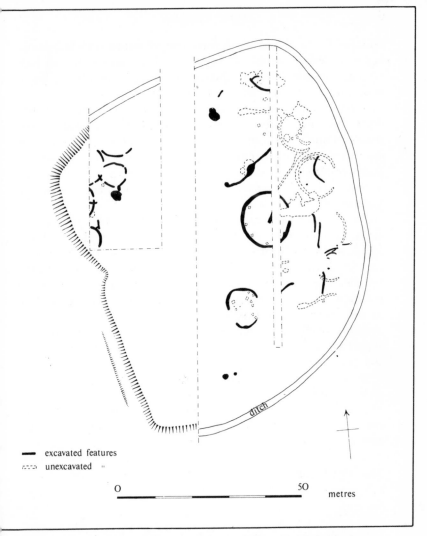

excavated features
unexcavated "

O   5O
                                        metres

4. Plan of the Iron Age settlement at Colsterworth (Lincs.)

represented here at the time of the Roman conquest and no
doubt earlier. West and north of the Trent in Nottinghamshire virtually nothing is yet known about the character of
late Iron Age settlement since the basic field-work has not
been done. In Leicestershire (outside Leicester itself)
occasional finds of Iron Age C pottery and metalwork have
been recorded, e.g. at Burrough Hill, Loughborough, and

Oadby. Rutland and north Northamptonshire are less informative, although finds of numerous Iron Age coins at Kettering, and still more at Duston, are suggestive indications of major settlements.

Little can yet be usefully said about the pattern of late Iron Age settlement, but some comment is needed on the kinds of settlement so far revealed. Since few of the hill-forts have been examined extensively, it is impossible to say what form occupation took within them in the century before the Roman arrival. Breedon Hill (Leics.) has, however, produced very little in the way of Iron Age C material[1][2] and seems not to have figured prominently in the political geography of the tribe at this time. Attention thus turns towards the other hill-forts in the south-western part of the canton. In at least one of these, Burrough Hill (Leics.), Iron Age C occupation has been briefly attested, and the need for more work here is pointed out. There is as yet no trace of great *oppida* like Prae Wood, Silchester or Camulodunum on Coritanian territory or indeed anything which remotely resembles the defensive dykes of such settlement complexes. The largest settlements yet recorded, sites like Dragonby, Ancaster and Old Sleaford, appear to be much smaller and more tightly nucleated. None is yet known to have possessed defences of any kind. Next in size come communities of a few families, like Colsterworth, and finally the single homestead, such as Tallington and possibly Rampton (below, p.95).

Finally, before leaving the Iron Age tribe, the evidence of the later Coritanian coinage may be briefly reviewed.

The evidence of Iron Age coinage[1][3]

The earlier groups of coins which can be distinguished as the mintages of Coritanian rulers bear no inscriptions, and thus have little to tell us beyond what has already been noted. Later series, probably dating from the very end of the first century B.C. down to the Roman invasion, are inscribed, and although the precise significance of the inscriptions cannot be established beyond question, they do prompt some thoughts about the political organization of the tribe. The coin-legends in question are as follows:

Obv.	Rev.	
	AVN	AST
	ESVP	ASV
	VEP	CORF
	VEP	
DVMNO	TIGIR	SENO
VOLISIOS	DVMNOCOVEROS	
VOLISIOS	DVMNOVELLAV	
VOLISIOS	CARTIVEL	

Those with two words on the reverse only, presumably the first parts of longer names, appear to be earlier in date than those with names on both the obverse and reverse. It is not certain whether the coins inscribed DVMNO TIGIR SENO carry three names or only two. *Tigirsenos* is an acceptable Celtic name, so that two names only may figure on these coins.

Now to the interpretation of the legends. Elsewhere on the pre-Roman coinages of Britain, when two names occur on the same coin, there is often good evidence that there was a dynastic link between the two. For instance, the sons of Commius placed their father's name as well as their own on their issues. Possibly, therefore, the coins with DVMNO and VOLISIOS on the obverse can be explained in this way, the senior member of the family being named on the obverse, and his son on the other side. Equally possible is the notion that Volisios and Dumno . . . were paramount chiefs, the names with which they are paired being those of local subservient kings. Difficulties arise, however, when we try to fit the paired reverse legends of the earlier coins, AVN AST, ESVP ASV, VEP CORF, into such a scheme. These can be more convincingly interpreted as the names of dual rulers or magistrates, who included coining as one of their privileges. No one will claim to have worked out the true solution when there are so many unknown factors, and where our evidence is so incomplete, but it might be suggested that AVN AST, ESVP ASV and VEP CORF were indeed paired magistrates.[14] Later, under different political conditions, a single leader, a Dumno . . . or a Volisios, united all the Coritani under his rule, but local *reges* continued to exercise power over individual kinship-groups and were allowed to put their names on the reverses of their coins. This will account for TIGIRSENO, DUMNOCOVEROS, DUMNOVELLAV, and CARTIVEL. This explanation would accord quite well with the fact that in the early decades of the first century A.D., if not earlier, we now know of three or four principal centres of the Coritani: Leicester, Old Sleaford, Dragonby and perhaps Ancaster. These places could represent the centres of kinship-groups within the tribe, each with its own king or chieftain. Where the paramount king may have resided can only be guessed at, but the claims of Leicester, later to become the Roman centre of administration, are strong. The neighbouring Iceni, Allen has recently suggested,[15] may also have made a move towards paramountcy towards the end of the period of British independence.

Several aspects of the coinage are still problematic. The chronology, in particular, is still vague. It is worth considering whether some of the latest issues, particularly those with the obverse legend VOLISIOS, might not have been struck after 43. Very few of the VOLISIOS coins have actually been found in the Coritanian area. The great bulk of them have derived from the south Yorkshire hoards mentioned above and they might therefore be the mintages of a chieftain who had decided to move north when the Romans occupied Coritanian territory.

The geography of the civitas Coritanorum

No direct evidence bearing on the boundaries of the Roman *civitas* has ever come to light, and it is extremely unlikely that it ever will. In the absence, therefore, of the specific testimony which literature and inscriptions alone can give, we can do no more than indicate the broad outline of the administrative unit which was formed out of the Iron Age tribe, confessing ignorance when we must on the detailed picture. It must at the outset be admitted that along the entire tribal frontier, except where this is fashioned by the sea-coast, we are adopting a boundary rather than redis-covering the original limits. A start may be made by considering the general problems posed by tribal boundaries, before passing on to the information provided by archaeology and by the sole literary source, the second-century astronomer-geographer Ptolemy.

It is a general but probably false assumption that the Iron Age tribes of western Europe *always* had *clearly* defined boundaries. It is a striking fact that many tribal societies in historical times often had no clearly marked and undisputed frontiers against their neighbours. Such peoples often only became conscious of their bounds when their land came under external threat. In Professor Mair's words,[16] 'People who cannot write do not draw maps, and so they may not know where their boundaries are until there is a fight about them. But they may still have a strong conviction that certain territory is theirs and nobody else's.' Another factor which will have had a bearing on the extent of land claimed by a tribe or a kinship-group at any one time is the Celtic system of clientship. A warrior or a minor chief could presumably transfer his allegiance and his land from one leader to another in accord with changing circumstances. Thus a king who enjoyed outstanding prestige through his success in warfare would build up a considerable following of warrior-nobles and the extent of the land over which he might claim a measure of control would increase during his time of fortune. On his death, there might be a drastic realignment of loyalties, his erstwhile followers now splitting up into rival cabals or attaching themselves to another tribal leader whose star was in the ascendant. In circumstances like these, it is plainly impossible to insist that the land held by a pre-Roman tribe in Britain was a fixed and inalienable unit. Although there will have been a stable core to the tribal land, on its fringes the territory will have been amoebic in character.

Ancient writers are not very informative about how barbarian tribes distinguished their territory from that of their neighbours. What evidence there is does not pertain to Britain. As is to be expected, such obstacles to passage as major rivers, forests, hill-ranges and marshes were often employed in this way. It cannot be assumed, however, that even large rivers *normally* divided the territories of different tribes. The truth of this is particularly evident in Free

Germany during the Roman Iron Age, where both banks of such major streams as the Weser, Elbe, Oder and Vistula were often held by the same peoples. As a general rule, it is much more likely that where rivers were easily passable by ferries or fords those streams united peoples rather than divided them, and that the same settlers thus held land on both banks, taking full advantage of the more accessible and more easily workable alluvial soils. Artificial demarcation of tribal land in western Europe is mentioned very rarely[17] and was probably exceptional.

On turning to the archaeological evidence, the category of finds which might seem to promise most on the extent of the Coritani is the Iron Age coinage now generally attributed to them. While this evidence certainly deserves attention, however, its value is limited. Although these coins (the mintages of chiefs, it will be remembered, and not tribal issues)[18] will normally have circulated within the tribal area, the evidence of their find-spots is not precise enough to enable a sharp definition of the limits of tribal land. But although the distribution pattern of the coins cannot be viewed as a wholly reliable guide to the extent of the Coritani, it does at least give a safe indication of where the core of their territory lay. Broadly speaking, the coins argue for a tribal heartland in what is now Lincolnshire, Rutland, Leicestershire and Nottinghamshire.[19] To the north and west of the Trent Valley, in an area where Iron Age settlement was probably fairly sparse, Coritanian coins are rare. To the south, the find-spots extend to the valley of the Nene, mingling there with larger numbers of the later coins of the Catuvellauni. To the west, towards the Cornovii, and south-west, towards the Dobunni, very few coins have yet been recorded.

The later Catuvellaunian bronze coinage offers a little assistance in determining the border between Catuvellauni and Coritani. Bronze coinage, since it was more closely tied to a market economy than gold and silver, had a much more local distribution. The later bronze coins, of Cunobelin especially, extend northward into Northamptonshire but no further than the watershed between Nene and Welland. North of this line they occur only occasionally, at Leicester, South

Ferriby and Market Overton. Taken all in all, then, the coins suggest that the Coritani were a tribe of the Trent basin, Lincolnshire and the northern part of the Midland plain. On this evidence, the northern and western borders remain uncertain, but the southern boundary appears to lie between the Welland and the Nene.

The only surviving Roman account from which anything can be deduced about the position of the tribe is the *Geographia* of Ptolemy, and that fact is enough to make this work claim our close attention.[20] As it happens, however, Ptolemy does not offer much real help. Drawing on first century sources, Ptolemy locates the Coritani, or the Coritavi as some of the manuscripts have it, to the east of the Cornovii, and assigns the two places *Lindon* and *Rhage* (*Ratae*) to them. He also mentions a place called *Salinae* and assigns it to the Catuvellauni. The co-ordinates he gives for *Salinae* locate it near the Wash, i.e. in an area where salt-making was certainly going on in the early Empire. On the face of it, this looks as if the Catuvellauni were in possession of south Lincolnshire and the adjacent Fenland margins. The point is so important that it will be well to remember the quality of our source. That there are gross mistakes and corruptions in the manuscripts of Ptolemy is a notorious fact and it would be unwise to build much of an edifice upon his siting of *Salinae*. There are three possible explanations for the anomaly. First, as Rivet[21] has pointed out, *Salinae* is located by Ptolemy at the appropriate distance from London to coincide with Droitwich (Worcs.), which is certainly the *Salinis* of the Ravenna Cosmography. The geographer thus may have placed it to the east instead of to the west of London. Secondly, it must be noted that something is sadly wrong with Ptolemy's latitudes, since he places *Salinae* in the same latitude as *Verulamium*, and *Verulamium* in the same latitude as Leicester! If one Catuvellaunian site could be wrongly located, so could another. Thirdly, there is the possibility that *Salinae* has been correctly located but assigned to the wrong tribe.

On this point, then, we must disagree with our source. The inhabitants of south-east Lincolnshire cannot have formed part of the Catuvellauni, since they must have been cut off from their neighbours to the south, until the second century at least, by the barrier of Fens. Either Ptolemy is here perpetuating an error in his sources or has created one of his own. In any event it plainly is an error. All Lincolnshire belonged to the Coritani.

We are left with the no less opaque evidence of Iron Age pottery and metalwork. The demonstration that the north-east midlands shared an Iron Age C culture with the south-eastern parts of the island has shattered the specious precision of the distinction which could plausibly be drawn ten years ago, on the evidence of the distribution of 'Belgic' pottery and bronzes, between an Iron Age C Catuvellaunian culture and the backward, possibly Belgic-influenced Coritani. With that lesson learned, it seems wise to keep an open mind about the extent of Iron Age C material northward and westward from the Trent valley. It may seem at present tempting to view the Trent as a cultural divide between the upland Brigantes and lowland, Iron Age C Coritani, but the truth is that we have hardly any idea of the character of Iron Age settlement in Nottinghamshire west of the Trent. It may yet prove to have had an Iron Age C strain. Even if it is ultimately shown that it did not, a cultural division of this kind need not in any case reflect a division between tribes or other units of population.

Having thus reviewed the evidence, we can turn to the boundaries which are to be adopted. It will be obvious from what has already been said that only general agreement with them is to be expected.

It has already been observed that the distribution of Coritanian coins suggests that the Iron Age tribe, and the later *civitas*, extended at its furthest no further south than the valley of the Nene. In that valley coins of the Catuvellauni are found in fair quantity, and these increase in relative quantity further south. So far as this category of evidence goes, therefore, it indicates that Catuvellaunian writ ran in this river valley, and thus presumably both sides of the stream were in the hands of this tribe. The border between the Coritani and the Catuvellauni may therefore have run along a line between Nene and Welland. It may not be too fanciful to see the rural Celtic shrines at Colley Weston and

Brigstock (Northants.)[22] as occupying a position on or near to the limits of the two tribal lands. Such a siting of temples has been suggested in the cases of certain tribes in Gaul.[23]

Towards the Cornovii in the west, the evidence of coinage and topography offers no help, and we are reduced to mere guesswork. Sir Ian Richmond's guess,[24] which cannot be greatly improved on, was that Cannock Chase and the hills of south Derbyshire were the border lands of the two peoples. The agriculturally hungry soils of Cannock Chase and Needwood Forest are likely to have been virtually empty in the Roman period as well as the Iron Age, and somewhere in this deserted countryside will have run the boundary between the two *civitates*. Probably, Ryknield Street ran close to the frontier, and in that case Wall (*Letocetum*) and Penkridge (*Pennocrucium*) will have been included among the Cornovii. Passing between Wall and Mancetter, the south-western boundary of the *civitas* presumably crossed the Fosse Way between High Cross (*Venonae*) and Chesterton, and led thence into the area of the watershed between Nene and Welland. Watling Street, later to serve as a boundary in middle and late Saxon England, and still forming the division between Leicestershire and Warwickshire, is adopted in this account as a convenient line of demarcation.

In the north we encounter little difficulty, the Humber clearly parting the Coritani from the Parisi of south-east Yorkshire. The north-western limits of Coritanian land, however, present perhaps the greatest problem of all. It has already been noted (above, p. 14) that there is reason for assigning the left bank of the Trent to the Coritani, and probably the sparsely peopled land of Sherwood Forest should also be included. But what of the country north of the Idle? Although Ptolemy gives no indication of how far north the Coritani extended, he does make it plain that the Brigantes laid claim to the Aire and Calder valley, since the place Camulodunum,[25] which can be identified as the Roman fort at Slack or the nearby hill-fort at Almondbury near Huddersfield, is assigned to them. The fact that the north Derbyshire hills had to be garrisoned throughout much of the Roman period indicates that their inhabitants were almost certainly a sept of the Brigantes, and on this ground the southern Brigantian border can be set between the rivers Don and Idle, and along the northern fringes of Sherwood Forest. Roman settlements in this area (below, p. 100) are much more akin to sites of an upland character in Derbyshire and south-west Yorkshire than to those of the Trent basin and must be assigned to the Brigantes. On the western side the siting of first century garrisons at Doncaster, Templeborough and Little Chester suggests that the Brigantes, which those garrisons were designed to hold in check, met the Coritani approximately along the line of Ryknield Street. To the west of this route the uplands of Derbyshire lay under military jurisdiction for much, if not all, of the Roman period, and thus can never have been part of the *civitas Coritanorum*.[26]

This, then, is the region to be covered in this survey (fig. 1). Two Roman documents help to fill out the details of tribal geography.

Apart from the work of Ptolemy already mentioned, the only Roman documents which provide information about the geography of the Coritanian region are those known as the Antonine Itinerary[27] and the Ravenna Cosmography.[28] The Antonine Itinerary is the more informative source for the East midlands and its evidence may therefore be considered first. Extracts from three of its routes are given and these are followed by comment on the Roman settlements with which the Itinerary place-names should be identified. These identifications were almost an after-dinner amusement in the eighteenth and nineteenth centuries, fantasies based on ludicrous etymologies being often entertained. There can be little debate about most of the Itinerary entries now.

Extract from Iter V

Durobrivae	MP	XXXV
Causennis	MP	XXX
Lindo	MP	XXVI
Segeloci	MP	XIIII
Dano	MP	XXI

Durobrivae is without question the walled settlement on

Ermine Street at Chesterton (Hunts.), at the northern gates of the Catuvellauni. This is not merely a deduction from the Itinerary distances. Inscriptions on locally produced mortaria record the name of the place as well as that of the potter: *Sennianus Durobrivis urit* and *Cunoard fecit vico Durobrivis*.[29] Fifty-six Roman miles to the north lay *Lindum*, plainly Lincoln on the evidence of etymology and of Roman inscriptions.[30] Between these two towns lay *Causennae*,[31] for long identified as the walled site at Ancaster. The Itinerary distances, however, 30 miles north of *Durobrivae* and 26 miles south of Lincoln, locate the place not at Ancaster but about six miles to the south, in the area of the junction of the Salt Way with Ermine Street. No settlement is known here, and presumably *Causennae* was no more than a posting-station on the main road. North of Lincoln, the route leaves Ermine Street and, following the Roman road now known as Till Bridge Lane, strikes north-west, reaching the Trent at *Segelocum*, the modern Littleborough. Thence, a 21-mile stretch brought the traveller to *Danum*, present-day Doncaster.

Extracts from Iter VI and Iter VIII

Iter VI		*Iter VIII*	
Tripontio	MP XII	*Lindo*	MP XIIII
Vennonis	MP VIIII	*Crococalano*	MP XIIII
Ratis	MP XII	*Margiduno*	MP XIIII
Verometo	MP XIII	*Vernemeto*	MP XII
Margiduno	MP XIII	*Ratis*	MP XII
Ad Pontem	MP VII	*Vennonis*	MP XII
Crococalano	MP VII		
Lindo	MP XII		

These two lists of sites mark out the same route in both directions, this covering the most northerly stretch of the Fosse Way. There are minor differences between the two *itinera*: *Iter VIII* omits *Ad Pontem*, and there are slight discrepancies between the two sets of mileages. Proceeding south-west from Lincoln, an interval of twelve miles brings us

to *Crococalana*, the modern hamlet of Brough.[32] Seven miles
further south lay *Ad Pontem*, now to be identified with fair
certainty with the settlement at Thorpe.[33] The bridge
referred to in the Roman name presumably lay across the
Trent, here swinging close to the west side of the Fosse Way,
and it appears to have carried a road leading north-west up
the valley of the Greet. A further seven miles along the Fosse
was *Margidunum*. This settlement[34] lies between the
modern villages of Bingham and East Bridgford, its site free
of medieval and later buildings, but now partially covered by
a large traffic roundabout. Continuing southward for a
further thirteen miles, *Vernemetum* is reached in the parish
of Willoughby on the Wolds, another Roman settlement
which lay largely in open fields before the coming of the
modern motorway. The Roman place-name[35] implies the
existence in or near the settlement of a native shrine or
sacred grove, the Celtic word for the latter being *nemeton*.
From here, *Ratae*, the tribal capital at Leicester, is thirteen
miles distant, and thereafter follow *Venonae* (High Cross)
and *Tripontium* (Churchover),[36] the latter marking the start
of a diversion from the Fosse Way on to the Watling Street.

The Ravenna Cosmography repeats a little of this information, two routes being of particular interest here:

Deva Victrix	*Durobrisin*
Veratinum	*Lindum Colonia*
Lutudarono	*Bannovalum*
Derbentione	

A further two place-names from this source are to be placed
in our area, *Ratecorion* and *Aquis Arnemeze*. *Ratecorion* and
Durobrisin are clearly garbled forms of *Ratae Coritanorum*
and *Durobrivae* respectively. But some of the other places
mentioned are otherwise unattested. The settlement called
Bannovalum must be sought somewhere in Lincolnshire,
perhaps at Horncastle or Caistor, where late Roman defensive
systems still survive to impress the visitor with their massive
character. The name probably means 'Peak Strength', and
thus Caistor would fit the bill better.[37] The site with the
intriguing name *Aquis Arnemeze*, which can be expanded on
Professor Richmond's suggestion to *Aquae Arnemetiae*,[38]

must be situated somewhere in Derbyshire, and since *Aquae* implies thermal springs, it is clearly Buxton — a known spa and Roman site[39] — that is intended. This may be another name containing the element *nemeton*, thus possibly indicating a native religious centre in the Derbyshire hills. The other place-names contributed by the Ravenna list also lie in the western districts. The most interesting are *Derbentione* and *Lutudarono*. The former must be Little Chester in the northern suburbs of Derby, by the river Derwent, the Celtic name for which has been transferred by the Romans to their fort-site.[40] *Lutudarono* (better known as *Lutudarum* on the evidence of inscriptions on lead ingots) cannot be so precisely located, and since other evidence reveals that the place was the centre of the lead-mining industry, this is an unfortunate gap in our knowledge. The guess may be hazarded that it lay in the Wirksworth area of south Derbyshire.[41] Further west, probably on the road leading towards the Cheshire plain, lay *Veratinum*, a place not surely identified, but probably represented by Rocester or Chesterton (Staffs.).[42] This outline of tribal geography may end with a puzzle. The name Chesterfield should be indicative of an important Roman settlement about half-way between Little Chester and Templeborough. The earliest recorded forms of the place-name, *Cesterfelda* and *Cestrefeld*, appear to mean 'open country near or belonging to a fortification',[43] but of a defended site there is no trace. Nor has Chesterfield produced evidence to suggest that there was a considerable Roman settlement here.

2.

History: A.D. 43-367

Within a matter of weeks after the Roman army landed on
the south-eastern coasts of Britain, the British capital at
Camulodunum was in the hands of the invaders, and of the
two Catuvellaunian leaders one was dead, and the other,
Caratacus, had fled to the western parts of the island. The
invading forces had probably achieved rather more than their
initial objectives by the end of 43, and the subsequent
overrunning of the lowlands of England was carried through
with speed. So far as can be judged from our slight sources,
the tribes of eastern and central England put up no prolonged
or effective resistance. Serious British opposition, stimulated
and organized by Caratacus, was encountered only in the
west.

The Coritani do not figure in the surviving Roman
accounts[1] of the occupation of Britain between A.D. 43 and
about A.D. 70, and we therefore have no explicit information
about their response to the arrival of the Roman army on
their southern borders. This absence of specific literary
evidence is a severe drawback to our understanding of these
early years, and on the attitude of the tribe to the new power
controlling southern Britain the *lacuna* is one which is
unlikely to be filled by archaeology. Since virtually all our
information is archaeological, the most we can hope to
achieve is an outline picture of the early military dispositions,
and some idea of how these were later modified by the
occupation of new forts and by changes of garrison. Notable
advances have recently been made in our understanding of
the progress of the earliest campaigns in eastern England, and

a summary of these will provide a convenient framework within which fresh discoveries can be accommodated.

As has already been noted, the immediate reaction of the Coritanian leaders to the Roman arrival is unknowable. Either they capitulated without a fight or they surrendered after only brief resistance, for by a very early date — 47 at the latest and probably by about 45[2] — much of the territory of the tribe was garrisoned by a network of forts based on the two great routes, the Ermine Street and the Fosse Way. The fact that this large tribe is mentioned by neither of the two historians whose accounts have come down to us, Tacitus and Dio, might be taken to mean that the Coritani offered no serious opposition to the advance. This argument, however, is by no means conclusive, for Dio does not mention many tribes in any case, and the crucial passages of Tacitus' *Annales* dealing with the invasion and its aftermath are lost. Nevertheless, it may reasonably be surmised that there were circumstances in which the Coritani, like their neighbours the Iceni of Norfolk, may have been prepared to accept alliance with the Romans, or even subjection to them. Both the Iceni and the Coritani must have viewed with some alarm the extension of Catuvellaunian power over the south-east midlands during the early decades of the first century A.D.,[3] and thus the rapid collapse of that formidable kingdom under Roman attack will have brought relief to both tribes. Further, the Coritani had on their northern borders the Brigantes, an aggressive people who were certainly powerful enough to exert pressure on their Lowland neighbours. To the Coritani, therefore, as to the Iceni, the Roman coming perhaps did not seem the disastrous event it clearly was for the Catuvellauni.

The army group entrusted with the job of occupying the eastern parts of England consisted of the Ninth legion (*Legio IX Hispana*) and an unknown, though sizeable, number of auxiliary troops, both cavalry and infantry. Marching-camps, which are the works most likely to belong to the earliest phase of campaigning, are still poorly represented. Large examples of these are known at Holme near Newark, and at Newton on Trent (Lincs.).[4] These lie close to the east bank of the Trent and probably mark the passage of an army in a very early penetration of the valley (fig. 5). Information about more permanent works is a little more extensive. Two large forts, at Longthorpe and Newton on Trent,[5] have been revealed by the air photographs of Dr St. Joseph and excavation in that at Longthorpe confirms that it at least must be dated to the years immediately following 43. The entire outline of Longthorpe has been traced from air photographs and its area can be assessed at almost 11.3 ha. Enough of the perimeter of Newton is known to make it certain that its area must be in the region of 10.1 ha. The defensive plans of these two sites are so close to each other as to suggest that they were the work of the same unit at about the same time. Newton has not yet been examined, but Longthorpe has yielded something of its plan to Professor Frere and Dr St. Joseph.[6] Its north gate had a double portal flanked by two towers, in the manner of the Great Casterton fort, described below (p. 24). By the side of the road leading to this gate lay a timber granary about 33.6 m. long, and the ground between the granary and the north-west angle of the fort was occupied by a large courtyard structure bounded on three sides by a corridor but open towards the *intervallum.* The purpose of this building is not clear. The evidence of pottery so far found indicates a foundation-date of shortly after 43. By about 60 the fort had been reduced in size, to about 5.6 ha., the new work occupying the centre of the old.[7] The reduced work was apparently a hasty improvisation: it may well belong to the years 60-1.

These large forts are matched by others of the pre-Flavian period in western Britain (e.g. at the Clyro (Herefords.) and Kinvaston (Shropshire)). They are large enough to have housed about half a legion, or a substantial detachment of legionaries together with auxiliary troops, and they presumably served as the temporary bases or the winter quarters of forces engaged in active campaigning at a time when there was still a need to maintain flexibility in the face of a changing situation.

The main brunt of garrisoning the territory fell upon the auxiliary forces and the ultimate aim of the student of this period of Romano-British history must be to reconstruct as nearly as possible the entire scheme of garrisons. There is a

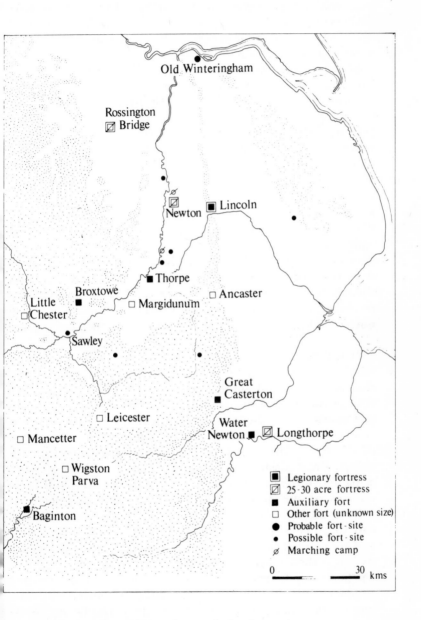

Old Winteringham

Rossington
Bridge

Newton

Lincoln

Thorpe

Broxtowe

Little
Chester

Margidunum

Ancaster

Sawley

Great
Casterton

Leicester

Water
Newton

Longthorpe

Mancetter

Wigston
Parva

Baginton

■ Legionary fortress
◩ 25-30 acre fortress
■ Auxiliary fort
□ Other fort (unknown size)
● Probable fort-site
• Possible fort-site
∅ Marching camp

0   30 kms

5. Early military sites on Coritanian territory

long way to go. Relatively few of the known forts have produced a satisfactory quantity of dating evidence, and the complete plan of none has yet been established. No doubt others still remain to be found.

Shortly after the invasion of Coritanian land a series of garrisons was strung out along Ermine Street, at intervals of between 24 and 40 km. (fig. 5). The sites of three can be located precisely, at Water Newton (Northants.),[8] Great Casterton (Rutland)[9] and Ancaster (Lincs.).[10] The sites of others can be reasonably guessed at. It is difficult to believe that the superb position which Lincoln offers was not immediately seized by the invading forces, and although no structural traces of any fort earlier than the Neronian legionary base have been recorded, it must be remembered that a large part of the upper town has never been explored and that very little has been seen of the earliest levels anywhere on the site.[11] No likely fort can be identified on the stretch of road between Lincoln and the Humber, but on the south shore of the estuary a site at Old Winteringham has produced timber buildings and associated Claudio-Neronian pottery. These could belong to a supply base serviced by the fleet.

It will be noticed that the Ermine Street forts are sited in relation to strategic points, such as river-crossings and road-junctions, and thus, Lincoln apart, are not tactically strong. Ancaster is overlooked from higher ground to north and south. Water Newton, too, guarding the Nene crossing, sacrifices tactical advantage in its siting near the flood-plain of the river. This is also true of the best known fort of this group, Great Casterton, which was positioned on a gentle slope above the crossing of the little river Gwash (fig. 6). The remains of this fort are worth close attention, since they offer a still rare instance of the complete circuit of a Claudian fort together with many details of its defensive arrangements and its gates. The discovery of this outstanding early fort is owing to the drought of 1959, and to the air photography of Dr St. Joseph. The exceptionally dry conditions of that summer resulted in the appearance of strikingly clear crop-marks, which revealed virtually the entire layout of the defensive ditches and, as a bonus, the fact that the fort had

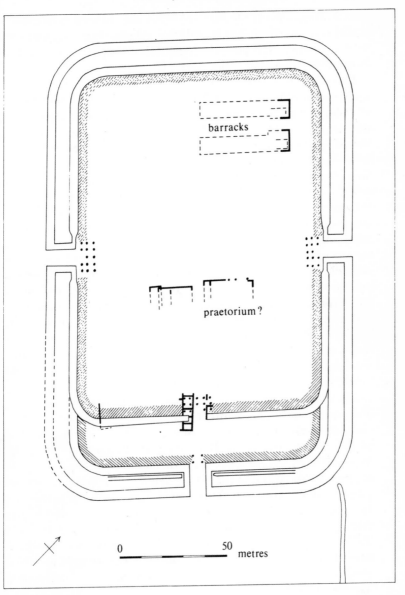

6. Plan of the Claudian and later fort at Great Casterton (Rutland)

passed through at least two periods of occupation.[1][2] Excavation confirmed this and showed that the original fort, 2.4 ha. in area, had later been reduced in size to 2.05 ha. by shortening the longer sides.

The defences of Fort 1 consisted of a rampart of limestone-rubble, revetted front and back by turf, and a pair of evenly spaced ditches cut into the natural rock, defining a platform or ravelin 7.6 m. to 8.3 m. wide. The rampart had been almost obliterated by ploughing, but it might be estimated to have stood some 4.6 m. high and to have been topped by a timber sentry-walk and breastwork. The purpose of the broad space between the twin ditches was that of a fire-trap, designed to entice an attacker across the slight obstacle of the outer ditch to within killing range of missiles thrown from the rampart. If the onrush of the enemy took him as far as the inner ditch, he would find that a much more formidable obstacle — and he would now be within a range where defenders would find it easier to strike home than to miss. On retreating under fire, the outer ditch, with its concealed and near-vertical outer face, was now a serious impediment. Defences incorporating a fire-trap are known in several other first century forts in Britain, and the overall resemblance between these indicates a common source, perhaps an official manual on the construction of military defences.

Three gates were provided for this fort, one in each of the long sides, and a third in the side looking towards the river. Only the latter could be completely excavated, and it proved to be of a simple type. Four upright timbers served as the framework of a tower, 4.1 m. wide and 3.7 m. deep. The first storey of this tower probably carried a sentry-walk across the gate-opening at the same level as the top rampart, and above that, a second staging may have afforded a higher vantage-point and fighting platform. Between the fort and the river lay an annexe, bounded on at least one side by a shallow ditch. Here, the watering activities of the garrison, any mounts it might have had, and its baggage animals, would have been carried on.

There has been no systematic examination of the interior of this fort, or of its successor, and therefore little is known about the arrangement of internal buildings. In these circumstances discussion of the original garrison at Great Casterton cannot go far, but there is the suspicion that legionaries may have been quartered here, perhaps temporarily in the early years.[13] Very little stratified pottery has been recovered from either fort, but the dating of the earliest coarse ware and a few samian ware sherds supports an opening date for the occupation within a few years of 43.

At a later date, probably after 70, nearly an acre at the south end of Fort 1 was cut off by a cross-ditch and an accompanying rampart. The new line of defence contained a wider gate than that which it replaced, its double portal of a 7.1 m. span being flanked by a pair of timber towers, each of which was framed by nine uprights. Still less of the internal planning is known than in the earlier fort, but it is apparent that a complete rearrangement was made, the old structures being systematically demolished to make way for the new, and also that the Fort II buildings are more widely spaced than their predecessors, suggesting a substantially reduced garrison-force. These changes were earlier linked with re-grouping of forces in this region occasioned by the revolt of the Iceni and Trinovantes in A.D. 60-1, but the slight evidence of pottery indicates a date of after 70.[14] Shortly afterwards, the garrison was finally withdrawn and the site levelled.

No other Claudian forts are known for certain, but several sites where military occupation is attested at some undefined pre-Flavian date may be noted here, since some may ultimately prove to have been founded in the period of invasion. Leicester, long suspected to be the site of an early fort, is now known to have been occupied by the army in the Claudio-Neronian period. A length of ditch of military pattern beneath the eastern quarter of the later town is the first certain clue to its position.[15] At Thorpe-by-Newark (Notts.) a small fort only about 0.8 ha. in area belongs to the same period, although its date is uncertain.[16] Mancetter (Warwicks.) was also the site of a fort,[17] though details of its layout are still elusive. Other possible sites are Willoughby (Notts.) at the half-way position between Leicester and *Margidunum*, Newark near the confluence of Devon and Trent,[18] Brough (Notts.), the find-place of a cheek-piece of what was probably a first century parade helmet,[19] and Horncastle (Lincs.).[20] Recent excavation has added a small fort at Wigston Parva on Watling Street, less than a mile from the junction with the Fosse Way at High Cross.[21] Much more work is needed on all these sites. Several may yet prove to be Neronian, and some may not be forts at all.

Although we cannot yet grasp all the details of the arrangement, it is becoming plain that the north-eastern sector of the early frontier was drastically remodelled in the decade between A.D. 50 and 60. The dating evidence from forts is still too slight to allow speculation about which governors were responsible for the work. At present we can go no further than to suggest that the years from A.D. 55 to 60, and perhaps continuing for a few years after that time, seem the likeliest period, i.e. the governorships of Didius Gallus, Q. Veranius and Suetonius Paullinus.

The first major change among the garrisons concerns *Legio IX Hispana*. Longthorpe I appears to have been abandoned by about A.D. 60, and about the same time a new legionary base was established at Lincoln. Early accounts of Roman Lincoln had assumed that the fine hill-top site overlooking the marshy valley of the Witham had been occupied by a legionary fortress, and excavation since 1943 has demonstrated that this was indeed so, the defences of the fortress being coincident with those of the later *colonia* on all four sides.[22] The associated finds of pottery were originally interpreted as indicating a start for the occupation of before A.D. 47: recent re-examination of this evidence now suggests an opening date of about A.D. 60.[23] The size of the fortress, 18.2 ha., is somewhat smaller than other legionary bases in first-century Britain, but is probably large enough to house an entire unit of about 5,000 men. This reuniting of parts of the same unit in a single base presumably indicates an important change in strategy. The period of campaigning on Coritanian soil was now well and truly over: there followed a regrouping, which, for the time being, was intended to contain the Brigantes.

Knowledge of structural remains of the Lincoln fortress is limited to the defences and one of its gates. The rampart is something of a rarity in Roman Britain, being fronted by a timber palisade, which was inserted in a rock-cut foundation-trench. The bank was revetted at the rear by a low timber wall and its base rested on timber strapping or corduroy. In front lay at least one ditch with the familiar V-shaped profile and cleaning channel. The Lincoln rampart is of a type which is much commoner in other provinces, especially Germany. Turf-revetted banks appear to have been the normal method of rampart construction employed by the army of occupation in Britain.[24]

The frontier system established in the early years of occupation was a deep zone of forts, its front aligned on the valleys of the Trent and Severn. Threading through this zone ran the Fosse Way, the main lateral line of communication in the frontier arrangements of the first governor of Britannia, Aulus Plautius. The Fosse Way forts in this region have not yet produced much evidence for their history. The site at *Margidunum* (Notts.) was certainly occupied by the Roman army during the early decades, but probably not as early as was deduced by its first excavator, Dr Felix Oswald. He argued that a fort was established here before A.D. 47 and interpreted the visible polygonal defensive system as that of a Claudian earth fort, later converted into stone.[25] These defences are now known to date from the late second century and are clearly to be related to the later civilian settlement on the Fosse Way, and not to an early military base.[26] There can be no doubt, however, that the considerable mass of pre-Flavian pottery and a few finds of specifically military equipment recovered from *Margidunum* mark the approximate position of a fort, of which no structural trace has yet been identified. The slightly higher ground to the north of the area so far excavated appears the natural place for it. The unit in garrison here left behind abundant evidence of iron-smelting activities, in the form of many pits containing slag.[27] The raw material had presumably been derived from deposits of iron-stone in Lincolnshire and Leicestershire. None of the abundant dating evidence from *Margidunum* need be as early as the governorships of Plautius and Scapula. A foundation date of A.D. 55/60 may now be regarded as certain for this military post.[28]

To the north of the Coritanian frontier sector, Roman diplomacy originally aimed at avoiding an occupation of the rugged hill country of northern Britain. Rome here placed her trust in the ability of the Brigantian queen, Cartimandua, to hold together all her warriors in a policy of co-existence with the Roman state. On the one side, Brigantian autonomy was to be respected: on the other, Rome would gain a secure northern buffer against less tractable barbarians. The arrangement might have worked well if the Brigantes could have been unified in fact as well as in theory. A later linear frontier might then have linked the valleys of the Trent and Severn, leaving Staffordshire and Cheshire as the Romano-British *agri decumates*. But it was asking too much of an uneasy amalgam of kinship-groups. Roman hopes were not long sustained. The Brigantian warriors rallied behind the anti-Roman leader Venutius and a Roman occupation of the north became inevitable.

The outermost limits to which Roman garrisons were pushed before the conquest of the Brigantes was set in motion are difficult to define. It is certain that at least two forts were established in the broken and wooded country north of the middle Trent in Nero's reign, but neither has yet been extensively examined. A great opportunity was missed in 1938-9, when the potentially important fort of Broxtowe, in the northern suburbs of Nottingham, was largely engulfed in a housing estate. Parts of the site were hurriedly excavated, but those who did the work failed to realize the true character of the site.[29] Some of the pottery and coins recovered at the time still survive and they indicate an occupation which is unlikely to have started before A.D. 55/60. Recent re-assessment of the original excavation records[30] combined with trial-trenching, has raised the strong possibility that two or three occupation phases are represented at Broxtowe, and that the total area of one of the works is likely to have been in excess of 4.8 ha. If the site were now available for excavation. Broxtowe would be a magnet for the student of this period.

Another Neronian fort stood at Strutts Park, a mile north of the centre of Derby and occupying the heights immediately across the river Derwent from the Flavian fort at Little

Chester: this too has disappeared beneath modern houses, but enough coins and pottery have now been collected from the site to make a Neronian, and possibly a Claudian, occupation certain.[31] Other sites need further study before they can be fitted into the scheme. These include an earthwork underlying the little Flavian road-side fortlet at Pentrich (Derbys.),[32] half-way between Little Chester and Chesterfield, and an odd earthwork of 0.6 ha. on the Trent bank at Sawley (Derbys.), the lay-out of which bears some of the marks of military planning.[33] The slight dating evidence recovered from this work suggests the Roman period, but it is no more precise than that. Lower down the Trent, a fort of this date, if not earlier, is to be expected at Littleborough (Notts.), where the Lincoln-Doncaster road crosses the Trent. Gale and Horsley record an earthwork on the east bank of the river, but if this ever existed, all trace of it has vanished.[34] On the northern fringes of the tribe, Neronian occupation is attested at the fort of Templeborough (Yorks.), but the character of the early fort is indeterminate.[35] Another site which may tentatively be associated with the Neronian reorganisation is the recently discovered work of 9.3 ha. at Rossington Bridge,[36] four miles south-east of Doncaster. In a fort of this size, legionaries may be presumed to have played a role. Possible historical contexts are the occasions when Roman troops were sent to aid Cartimandua, and the governorships of Vettius Bolanus and Petillius Cerialis. The work of the land-based garrisons in the region of the lower Trent might well have been assisted by a detachment of the fleet. Although there is no certain trace of such a force, the potential value of a supply base on the Humber will not have escaped the High Command. Of known sites on the Humber shore, Old Winteringham[37] has produced pottery of the appropriate date and further work here might reveal the installations which were associated with such a base.

Early in the reign of Vespasian there came the long overdue advance into Brigantian territory, which was eventually to lead to total abandonment of the frontier zone established by Aulus Plautius and elaborated by his successors. In A.D. 71, *Legio IX Hispana* was advanced from Lincoln to York, being replaced at Lincoln by the newly raised *Legio II Adiutrix*. This move was accompanied by a reorganization of auxiliary garrisons. Now the Great Casterton fort was reduced in size to suit the needs of a smaller unit, and this change was shortly followed by complete abandonment.[38] *Margidunum*, Ancaster and Baginton were apparently given up at about the same time, and certainly by about A.D. 80. Agricola's garrisoning of the Pennines (A.D. 78-85) brought new forts to Brough-on-Noe, to Doncaster and probably to Buxton,[39] all of these lying beyond the limits of the tribal land. Within the territory, the only certain trace of a garrison is at Little Chester, where a fort of unknown size was built at the Derwent crossing on the opposite bank from the earlier fort.[40]

In common with the rest of Midland Britain, Coritanian territory has little military history from the late first century until the early fourth. There is no certain evidence that the region was visited by major alarms and excursions in the later second century, a period when the true magnitude of the military tasks imposed by the occupation of Northern Britain will have been brought home to the Roman High Command. By and large in Midland and Southern Britain, the second and third centuries are a field for the social and economic historian, not his military colleague. This was the period of major developments in agricultural settlement, in the life of towns and villages, and of the burgeoning of trade and industry. The history of the time is therefore implicit in the accounts of economic life given in Chapters 3, 4 and 5.

The only military garrison likely to have been maintained in the second century lay at Little Chester. Here, the Agricolan fort appears to have been succeeded by Hadrianic and later posts on the same site.[41] The defensive systems of none of these forts have been identified at any point, but timber buildings constructed in military style are unmistakeable evidence of the presence of the army. Still later, a stone-walled enclosure of 2.4 ha. dating from after the Antonine period was built. It is not clear whether these latest defences belong to a civilian settlement or to a fort. Their massive structure, incorporating a wall 2.74 m. wide, an earth rampart behind and the T-shaped arrangement of the internal streets, as reflected in the modern plan, points to the latter alternative. If the Little Chester fort was indeed occupied in the Hadrianic period, this would represent a divergence from the pattern of the history of other south Pennine forts. The fort at Brough-on-Noe, for example, appears to have remained unoccupied during the reign of Hadrian and throughout the early years of his successor Antoninus Pius, and to have received its next garrison after about A.D. 154. Little Chester was not, however, the only south Pennine fort to maintain a garrison throughout this period. The large fort at Templeborough, just outside Rotherham, a site now inaccessible beneath several feet of industrial slag, also seems to have been continuously occupied until the mid-second-century, while Melandra Castle, on the western slopes of the Derbyshire hills, was certainly held under Hadrian. Obviously much more work is required on these forts before we can begin to hope for clarification of what lay behind the treatment accorded to different garrison-posts.

If a fort was actually maintained at Little Chester from the late first century until the Antonine period, it follows that this part of Derbyshire will have been under direct military control and that its history, therefore, lies outside the scope of this book. It is now clear that the Peak district was under military supervision throughout most of the Roman period, being controlled by a garrison at Brough-on-Noe, and it is possible that the two forts at Brough and Little Chester were the nodal points of a patrol-system by which the whole of this intractable area was policed.

The withdrawal of military garrisons from the tribal territory in the late first century implies that government of the region was now formally handed over to tribal authority, embodied in the *ordo*, or municipal senate, of the *civitas*. Thus Leicester, which as we have seen was most probably one of the main centres of the Iron Age tribe, became in the last years of the first century the hub of tribal organization, the meeting-place of the *ordo decurionum*, the repository of municipal records, and, no doubt, the residence of many of the more wealthy and influential Coritani. A different kind of official urban foundation came into being at about the same time. Before A.D. 96,[42] a *colonia* was founded at

Lindum on the site of the old legionary fortress, now demolished to make way for the new city. The precise date of the foundation is not recorded. *Legio II Adiutrix* had left Britain by A.D. 92, appearing in Moesia in that year: its withdrawal from Lincoln may have occurred as early as 76-7. The charter of foundation will probably have been granted not long after the legion left and thus the colony may have been first laid out about A.D. 90.

The new city of *Lindum Colonia* was a veteran colony, housing ex-legionaries who were now awarded as their *praemia militiae* a grant of land, which they might work themselves, or of money, with which they might begin a career in business or trade. But early *Lindum*, like the earlier colony at *Camulodunum* (Colchester) and the slightly later foundation at *Glevum* (Gloucester), was not simply a community of ex-legionaries. Native Coritanian settlers, and other civilians, will have played their part in the early development of the city and in the exploitation of its territory. This native element may indeed have been more influential than the ex-soldiers in the early life of the new colony.[43] Many natives and immigrant civilians would already have settled close to the legionary fortress in order to make a living from the leisure-time spending of the soldiery — probably the most affluent members of the Romano-British population at this time. Some of these early settlers and *entrepreneurs* probably stayed behind in *Lindum* after the withdrawal of the legion and, if they prospered, their wealth would later be invested in agriculture.

The territory assigned to the new colony cannot be defined with any precision. Since so much of the land to the south-east and south-west of the city is marshy and cultivable only after extensive drainage, the *territorium* may well have extended far to the north and south along the more amenable limestone ridge, and to the north-west across the lowlands towards the Trent. A milestone found at the centre of *Lindum* records a distance of fourteen miles A L S.[44] This abbreviation has been expanded to read A L(indo) S(egelocum) — from Lincoln to Littleborough — and the further deduction has been made that *Segelocum* therefore lay on the territory of the colony. The expansion is difficult to accept without query, and even if it is accepted this particular piece of evidence is hardly cogent. It is, however, highly probable that the territory extended as far west as the Trent valley. To the south it may well have reached as far as Ancaster, and to the north perhaps almost to the Humber. Hardly anything is yet known about the pattern of farming settlement on the territory of *Lindum* at any date. Villas are conspicuously rare in the area about the city and it must be assumed that many of the veteran colonists and native *incolae* farmed their land from the city itself. Thirty-two km. to the south-west of the city lay the potentially fertile Vale of Belvoir, where humble farming settlements are now beginning to reveal themselves. It is not impossible that this rich but heavy land was first exploited by the power of Roman capital wielded from Lincoln (below, p. 100).

The factors governing the choice of Lincoln as a veteran colony have not, of course, been recorded for us by any Roman writer, but the suggestion of Sir Ian Richmond, that the selection of *Lindum* and of territory already converted to Imperial use was determined by the desire to deprive the Coritani of as little good land as possible, has much to recommend it. His words deserve to be quoted:

> The *colonia* was planted in a spot which had already been placed at the disposal of the Roman government by agreement or requisition for a legionary fortress and its *prata*. The area had thus been already acquired from the Coritani by early terms of alliance; and in substituting the *colonia* for the legionary fortress, the Roman government, while in effect making permanent their acquisition of territory, did so with as little fresh disturbance as possible.[45]

The chronological development of the towns and the larger villages is a subject about which hardly anything can yet be safely ventured, but by analogy with other areas of the province it is probable that the second century was a period of steady urban growth. The dating of town defences is an object much more easily attained and, with good reason, a great deal of attention has been paid to this aspect of the history of Romano-British towns. In the period A.D. 180-230, there are indications that several of the more important Coritanian towns and settlements received defences, with one exception for the first time. Only at Lincoln can earlier defences be claimed, and here it was the old timber-fronted rampart round the legionary fortress which did duty for the growing *colonia*. At a date which must be considerably later than about A.D. 180-90 — the date of a worn coin of Commodus found in the *colonia* rampart[46] — the first-century defences, now doubtless much weathered, were refurbished. The bank was greatly increased in size, and a stone wall added a few feet in front of the timber palisade. The latter could now be removed, and the space between it and the new wall filled up with rubble. The coin of Commodus is a clear indication that the new work cannot date from before the reign of Severus at the earliest, but how late in the third century it may be is still impossible to determine. Second-century bronze coins are frequently found in mid-third-century coin hoards, and at present the coarse pottery is of little help. As in many similar circumstances in Roman Britain, we are up against the major difficulty of being unable to distinguish clearly between the pottery of the later second century and that of the early third.

The town defences of Leicester also appear to date from the early third century, but it must be stressed that this judgement rests on very little stratified pottery.[47] The wall and the rampart are probably contemporary, and no sign of a defensive circuit antedating the wall has been observed, unless a timber palisade encountered on the south side finds its true historical context here. This palisade, which is undated, has only been noted at one point and thus it is by no means certain that it ever formed part of the town defences.

The defensive systems of two of the smaller settlements reveal a different structural sequence from that manifest in the two cities (fig. 7). Both *Margidunum* and Thorpe (Notts.) on the Fosse Way appear to have received simple earthwork defences, consisting of a bank and one or more ditches, before their stone walls, and the dates of both early systems are at present placed in the late second century. At *Margidunum* the stone wall was added to the earlier rampart at a date which remains unknown, while at Thorpe later

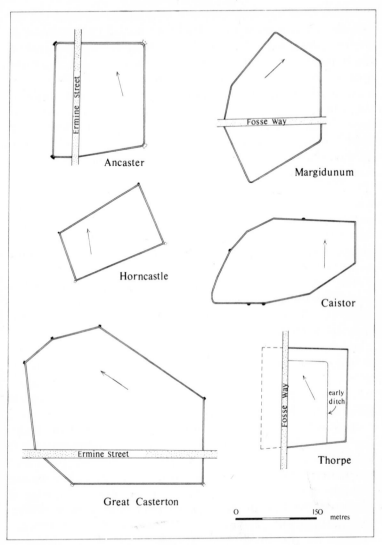

7. The defensive systems of 'small towns'

stone defences — perhaps of the fourth century — ignored the earlier circuit entirely.[48]

One of the first small towns in the province to be studied with the object of elucidating the structural history of its

defences was Great Casterton. The elongated plan of the
defences of this settlement, enclosing an 7.2 ha. area close to
Ermine Street, suggests that, unlike *Margidunum* and Thorpe,
the defences of Great Casterton were designed to enclose the
greater part of the settlement-area. Here, no defences in
earth-work antedating the construction of the town wall were
identified: rampart and wall were held to be contemporary.[49] Rather meagre dating evidence from the rampart
suggested to the excavators a date in the late second century,
or very early in the third,[50] but the cumulative evidence
from all parts of Britain for the erection of stone walls *after*
the reign of Severus, and in several cases after about
A.D. 250, indicates that the recovery of more stratified
pottery from Great Casterton is called for. It is inconceivable
that the settlement at Great Casterton was walled in stone
before such major towns as Lincoln, Leicester, Canterbury
and Verulamium.

The Ancaster circuit of defences, the plan of which was
finally established only in 1970, can be dated with unusual
precision. A small amount of pottery from below the bank
suggests a construction date of about or after A.D. 250. A
terminus ante quem — a rarity in Romano-British town
defences — is provided by five coins sealed between succes-
sive floors of a building erected over the tail of the rampart.
All five coins date from the decade 270-80, and the rampart
must therefore date from the period A.D. 250-80.[51]

The defensive systems of the other minor settlements are
less well known. The defences of Mancetter present problems
in their dating and even their plan has not yet been fully
elucidated. A stone-walled circuit was at some unknown date
erected, but there may have been an earlier defence in
earthwork.[52] The situation at Brough-*Crococalana* is still less
well defined. Here air photographs reveal two broad defensive
ditches to the north-west of the Fosse Way, apparently
cutting across earlier occupation represented by pits and
trenches of many kinds. The area enclosed by the ditches
may be roughly estimated at 2.8 ha. at least. Since no
controlled excavation has yet taken place at Brough, these
defences cannot be dated.[53] Recent work at Churchover-
Tripontium has revealed another ditched enclosure straddling

a main road, the area of this one being about 1.9 ha. Once again the date is uncertain. Several other settlements have not yet produced any clear sign that they were ever defended. These include Littleborough-*Segelocum*, Willoughby-on-the-Wolds-*Vernemetum*, and High Cross-*Venonae*.

The purpose of these small defended enclosures is a puzzle. It is often assumed that they were designed solely to protect the settlements themselves. There are, however, certain official functions which they might have performed. One of the most important of these is connected with the security of the main roads. In the late Empire roads had to be protected as well as maintained and small posts or *burgi* like those at *Ad Pontem, Crococalana* and *Tripontium could* have housed small garrisons of line-of-communication troops for this purpose. Another possible function is to provide protection of the *annona* as it was being carried towards store-houses in towns or forts. In the fourth century the *annona* was one of the most detested of state impositions. Protection of the goods and their collectors would almost certainly be needed.

Certain administrative changes were brought into effect in this period, and in so far as these involved the Coritani they must be discussed. In the reign of Septimius Severus (A.D. 193-211), or in that of his son and successor Caracalla (A.D. 211-17),[54] the province of Britain was divided into the two units *Britannia Superior* and *Britannia Inferior*. The geographical boundary between the new provinces cannot be drawn with any precision, but an inscription from Bordeaux,[55] set up by a man who was an official associated with the Imperial cult in the colonies of York and Lincoln, and dated to A.D. 237, reveals that both those cities lay in *Inferior*. It must be assumed that the entire *civitas Coritanorum* was included in that same province, along with Lindum and its territory. *Britannia Inferior* contained the garrisons of the northern frontier and its hinterland, and the inclusion of the rich agricultural region occupied by the Coritani was probably an attempt to make the new unit as nearly self-sufficient as possible.

After the restoration of Britain to the control of the central government in A.D. 296, the province of *Britannia Inferior* was itself divided into *Flavia Caesariensis* and

Britannia Secunda.[56] York and Lincoln were the capitals of
the new units, and it was *Flavia* which was centred on
Lincoln. The extent of the province is not recorded in, or
deducible from, any ancient source, but probably it included
all the territory of the Coritani and perhaps that of the Iceni
as well. Another important development in the administration of Roman Britain occurred during the third and fourth
centuries, viz. the granting of the right of self-government to
divisions of the existing *civitates*. It has, for instance, been
reasonably suggested that *Durobrivae* on the southern border
of the Coritani became the caput. of a new *civitas* carved out
of the northern reaches of the Catuvellauni.[57] A sub-division
of the Coritani appears to be specifically mentioned on a tile
recently found at Churchover — *Tripontium* (Warwicks.), in
an inscription incised before the tile was fired.[58] It runs

> ....] ITATIS CORIELSOLILIORUM [....
>>]   NIOM
>>]   M
>>]   CESOM

and the first line can best be restored as referring to the
civitas Corielsoliliorum. The centre of this otherwise
unknown community, we can surmise, was Churchover itself,
but the extent of its territory, if it possessed any, defies even
guesswork. It we accept the evidence of this tile — and it is
hard to see the *civitas Corielsoliliorum* merely as the *jeu
d'esprit* of some bored workman — there is no reason why
other administrative units or *civitates* should not have
escaped detection. Who were the Corielsolilii? Probably they
formed a division of the pre-Roman Coritani, which had
maintained its identity, perhaps as a *pagus*, under the Empire
and had then achieved a higher status. The case of the
Catalauni of Gaul provides an analogy.

The status of Leicester may also have altered during the
middle of the Roman period. Frere has already pointed
out[59] that in the Antonine Itinerary (a compendium of
several documents of various dates, brought together in the
early third century) it is precisely those towns which have
afforded proof of their thorough Romanisation, such as

Wroxeter, Canterbury and Leicester, that are mentioned without their tribal suffixes, as though they had been raised to the rank of chartered towns, probably *municipia*. Thus Leicester may have become a *municipium* during the second century, perhaps with the *ius Latii* under which the yearly elected magistrates became full Roman citizens.

Written sources and informative inscriptions are notoriously rare after about A.D. 220, and it is not until the upheavals at the end of the third century that it again becomes possible to write something approximating to history. Almost the only dated records of the mid- and late third century are the inscriptions on milestones. A surprisingly high proportion of the surviving milestones date from about A.D. 240 to 280, the reigns of Gordian III, Trajan Decius and Victorinus being particularly well represented. To a degree, of course, the commonness of milestones from this period reflects no more than the frequent changes of ruler. An emperor who survived for five years in the mid-third century was either remarkably fortunate or preternaturally alert. But allowing for this, it is evident that a good deal of attention was being given to the upkeep and repair of the main routes. Ermine Street shared in this programme of repair, as the milestones from Lincoln and *Durobrivae*[60] show. The latest date from the reign of Victorinus (A.D. 268-70). Again, shortly after A.D. 300 and during the reign of Constantine (A.D. 307-37), another large group of milestones, including one Coritanian instance from Ancaster,[61] attests official concern to maintain adequate communication.

By A.D. 314 it is almost certain that Lincoln was the centre of a Christian bishopric. In that year three British bishops, attended by a priest and a deacon, were present at the Council of Arles, these five men representing the metropolitan churches of the four British provinces. The text which records the British delegation runs as follows:

Eborius Episcopus de civitate Eboracensi provincia Britannia. Restitutus Episcopus de civitate Londiniensi provincia suprascripta. Adelphius Episcopus de civitate colonia Londiniensium. Exinde Sacerdos presbyter, Arminius diaconus.

(Bishop Eborius from York in the province of Britain. Bishop Restitutus from ?London in the afore-mentioned province. Bishop Adelphius from ?Lincoln. Thence (also) Sacerdos a priest and Arminius a deacon.)

The text is partially corrupt. Most probably *Lindiniensi* should be read following the name of Restitutus, or *Lindiniensium* after that of Adelphius, since *Lindum* was a provincial capital at this time.

From about 270, the south-eastern shores of Britain appear to have become increasingly vulnerable to raiding by sea-borne parties of Germans from the coast-lands of northern Europe. These raiding-parties were probably small and the effects of their marauding relatively limited, but the measures taken by those responsible for the defences of the island leave no doubt that the threat was seriously considered. The Roman response was the system of coastal forts and signal stations designed for co-operation with the fleet, generally known as the Saxon Shore.[62] In its fully developed form, which was achieved in all probability some years before A.D. 300, the system covered the coast from the Wash to the Solent. The Roman fleet may well have held the Lincolnshire stretch of the coast under surveillance, using the Humber as well as the Wash as a base, but, as we shall see, hopes of identifying the associated coastal installations cannot be high.

There are, however, two sites in east Lincolnshire, Caistor and Horncastle,[63] which can be plausibly connected with a system of defence against sea-borne raiders. Both sites have long been known to possess massive stone walls, with projecting bastions, of a design which became usual from the later third century onward, and which marks them out as of quite a different stamp from the other *places fortes* in the region. Neither site has yet produced reliable dating evidence for its defences, but certain constructional features offer guidance. At Horncastle and probably at Caistor too the bastions are of one build with the wall. If these places were towns, this fact should indicate that the entire defensive works were erected after A.D. 369, and formed part of Count Theodosius' reorganisation of town defences, for there is no good evidence that projecting towers were added to town-walls before that time. But if they were considerable civilian settlements or large villages, they would surely have been walled before this. The Horncastle defences, moreover, give away a clue that they are earlier than 369, since they incorporate a substantial earth rampart which is certainly contemporary with the wall and its bastions. Generally, the provision of prominent earth ramparts became infrequent after the mid-third century, and rare after the early fourth. Late-third-century town and fort walls in Gaul, to name the most conspicuous case, often omitted them altogether. A late fourth century example would be a distinct peculiarity. A date before A.D. 300 therefore seems more appropriate for Horncastle and probably for Caistor, and if this is accepted they will have been forts rather than walled civilian centres. The plans of the two sites contribute nothing to the discussion. The trapezoidal plan of Horncastle can be parallelled among forts and towns alike, and the same is true of the approximately oval circuit of Caistor.

Both sites cry out for further detailed study. It is astounding to recall that extensive sections of stone defensive works could still survive above ground and not be discovered and adequately recorded, as was the case with Caistor, until 1960. Here, the lower parts of at least three projecting towers are still visible, two on the south side, the other on the north.[64] The best preserved of those on the south side is 5.2 metres wide, projects about 3.05 m. from the curtain wall, and stands now to a height of about 2.13 m. Virtually all the facing blocks have been stripped away by stone-robbers, leaving the concrete and rubble core exposed. The tower on the north side preserves its original facing to a height of at least 1.37 m. — 1.52 m. so that it can be clearly seen that it is bonded into the wall-face and is thus contemporary with that structure. Since this tower occurs slightly east of the centre-point of the northern defences, it may be the eastern flanking tower of the north gate rather than a bastion. Buildings within the walls of both forts have not yet been revealed, but it is clear that both places had an extensive extra-mural settlement. At Horncastle this may have been concentrated some distance from the walls. At least one small dwelling outside the walls of Caistor was still occupied in the mid-fourth century.

If Horncastle and Caistor are accepted as forts, it follows that there were installations on the coast with which they were in contact, but, as has already been noted, severe coastal erosion since the Roman period[65] will almost certainly preclude discovery of any shore-forts or signal-posts which mây have existed. Later medieval documents make it plain that the coastal stretch between Mablethorpe and Skegness has suffered the worst damage in the transgression of the fifteenth century and later. No less than five medieval churches, together with much of the inhabited areas associated with them, have been destroyed by the sea, at Mablethorpe St. Peter's, Trusthorpe, Sutton, Chapel St. Leonard and Skegness. The last-named place is often quoted as a harbour of considerable importance before its destruction, following Leland's account[66] of what Skegness had lost before about 1540:

> To Skegness sumtyme a great haven toune . . . Mr Paynelle sayid onto me that he could prove that there was ons an haven and a towne wallid having also a castelle. The old toune is clene consumid and eten up with the se, part of a chirch of it stode a late. At low waters appere yet manifest tokens of olde buildinges. For old Skegness is noe builded a pore new thing.

Local legend has probably exaggerated the importance of old Skegness as a harbour,[67] but it is not impossible that Mr Paynelle's 'castelle' was indeed a fort of Saxon Shore type. Unfortunately, the real character of the lost sites of the Lincolnshire coast will probably never be known. The *a priori* case for late Roman garrisons and signal stations, however, remains strong. Since early-third-century forts were provided to protect the Thames estuary and the Wash,[68] it is at least likely that a similar measure was taken to cover the approaches to the Humber at about the same time. Grimsby would be an appropriate position for such a fort, but once more the answer to the question lies in the sea.

The chronology of barbarian raids on the eastern coasts which made defensive measures necessary has not been recorded for us, and archaeology has not yet provided much material to inspire speculation. The eastern side of Britain, including the territory of the Coritani, has produced a relatively large number of coin-hoards which close with issues dating from the years A.D. 270-2. Even allowing for the effects of financial insecurity upon the burial of hoards, the sharp rise in the number of savings-deposits concealed and not recovered in the period *c*.260 to 270 is probably due to swiftly executed raids by plundering war-bands. The main aim of such assailants at this date would be to grab as much portable loot as possible and get back to their ships before the nearest Roman community could raise a force of men to intercept them. The raiders would not be interested in walled towns and defended road-side posts, for their inferiority in numbers and equipment meant that they could never hope to carry on a siege. It was the vulnerable farms and villas which attracted them, particularly the villas, and it is here that we should expect to find evidence of their attacks. For two reasons we fail to do so. First, no more than four or five villas in the entire tribal area have been studied with the necessary care. Secondly, buildings largely constructed of timber — as is true of most villas — were naturally highly inflammable, and a domestic accident could be as devastating as a German raid. Several Coritanian villa sites show destruction-layers of ash and burnt timbers,[69] but in not a single case can it be asserted that the destruction was due to hostile action rather than an accidental fire. To take one instance, the villa at Norton Disney (Lincs.) was, in the view of its excavator, damaged in the late second century and again in the middle of the third.[70] But in the case of neither destruction is there sufficient evidence for the *deliberate* wrecking of the building and its contents, and in the absence of such evidence it must be assumed that the fire was caused accidentally. In the present state of our knowledge, archaeology has nothing to tell us on the subject, but it cannot be claimed that this field has been more than cursorily examined. For the present it can only be remarked that of those villas and other agricultural sites which have been recently examined, not one shows clear signs of having been devastated by enemy action. This is as true of the fourth century as of the third. The first half of the fourth century was the high summer of Romano-British agricultural prosperity, and there is no evidence from any source to suggest that it was seriously threatened by invaders until the 360s. Not even the disastrous years 367-9 have left any recognizeable traces in the excavated settlements. No destruction level certainly dating from those years can be identified in any town, villa or homestead in the region. And after 369 the picture is one of a prolonged decay rather than brief chaos.

3.

Communications and urban settlement

It is not proposed to describe in detail the entire system of roads and tracks in use in Coritanian territory during the Roman period. The principal routes which traversed the tribal territory and many of the links between the more important settlements are well established and are easily accessible to the reader in I.D. Margary's work *Roman Roads in Britain* and on the Ordnance Survey *Map of Roman Britain* (3rd ed. 1956). In the place of a descriptive text, a map is here offered incorporating those routes established as Roman and included in those works, together with a few stretches of road more recently traced for which a Roman origin seems probable (fig. 8). The major prehistoric trackways are also included on the map. These are likely to be forgotten amid the welter of information available on Roman roads, but they played their part in the communications of Roman Britain: some were still in use during the medieval centuries. It is hoped that the absence of a full text will not be taken to mean that the map represents the last word on the subject. Much remains to be learnt of the minor roads and *diverticula*, and even certain major routes could be clarified by further field-work.

In contrast to the road systems Roman canal systems are rarities in any part of the Empire. It is therefore all the more astonishing that the Lincolnshire Car Dyke and Foss Dyke, the longest Roman canal in western Europe and one of the most interesting field monuments in England, should never have been exhaustively studied or even adequately described. This brief account cannot do justice to this major work of

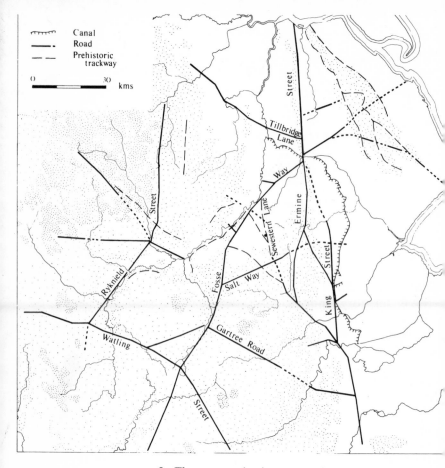

8. The communications network

Roman engineering. A full-scale survey of all the surviving works is sorely needed, to be followed by excavation on sites where something of its history is likely to be learned. Such a survey has now begun but its results will be slow to accumulate. For the present, it must be enough to describe the Dyke as it now reveals itself, and then to summarize what can be deduced about its functions.

The Lincolnshire Car Dyke is a great ditch[1] flanked on either side by a bank, running close to, and in some sectors actually along, the western edge of the Fenland from a point just to the east of Lincoln to the Nene at Peterborough. Here we will be concerned only with this canal between the

Witham and the Nene, but it will be borne in mind that south of the Nene a network of artificial channels and natural watercourses offered ready access for barges and small craft to the southern Fenland as far south as the Cam. The best known of these channels in the southern Fenland is the Cambridgeshire Car Dyke, or Old Tillage, which has been shown by Professor Clark's excavation at Coddenham to be of Roman origin.[2] To return to the Lincolnshire Dyke, a few subsidiary artificial channels run into it from the east and another major canal, the Foss Dyke, links the Witham immediately west of Lincoln with the Trent at Torksey. The Car Dyke has never been tested by excavation and thus there is no direct evidence for its Roman date. The Foss Dyke was on more than one occasion re-cut as a navigable channel in the post-medieval period and in consequence it must be imagined that much of the original cutting has been obliterated. There are, however, several sure indications that both works belong to the Roman period. First, fair quantities of Roman objects have been recovered from both their beds.[3] This is, of course, by no means conclusive, but the accumulation of evidence would be surprising if the work were post-Roman. Secondly, the Car Dyke figures in a number of medieval documents (generally as a boundary) and these demonstrate that it was certainly in existence by the late twelfth century.[4] Reclamation of the Fens had made little progress before 1200 and since the Dyke can only have come into existence during or after draining, it is with the Roman drainage that it must be associated. Finally, the scale of the work and the engineering capacity displayed in its construction point to Roman enterprise rather than to any medieval administration.

William Stukeley is often given the credit for being the first to point out that the Dyke was probably of Roman origin, but at least one earlier writer[5] had formed this opinion. To Stukeley, however, must be accredited the notion that the Car Dyke and Foss Dyke were designed to form links between navigable rivers, thus allowing passage of bulk cargoes — in his estimation cargoes of corn — from the Fenland to the Humber, and thence to York. In general terms, Stukeley's opinion still commands widespread

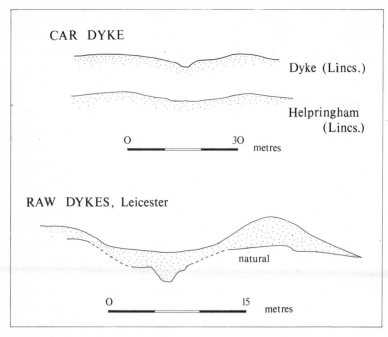

9. Sections across the Car Dyke and the Raw Dykes

support, although recent research suggests that stock rearing was at least as important as arable farming in large parts of the Fenland and that we should therefore add various animal products, especially hides and meat, to the grain.[6] Some of Stukeley's other surmises about the Dyke are of less worth, for instance his dating of it to the procuratorship of Catus Decianus (*c.* A.D. 60) on the evidence of modern place-names, and later to the reign of Carausius (A.D. 287-93) on similar evidence.

Since the last account of the course of the Dyke was published in 1872,[7] a brief description will not be out of place here (fig. 10). Close to the Witham, the Dyke has virtually disappeared and its junction with the river is unknown. From Potter Hanworth to Billinghay, it follows the contour of the slightly higher ground on the western Fen margin, crossing as it does several small streams running from west to east. This course entailed many bends and a

10. The Car Dyke east of Helpringham (Lincs.). The upcast banks show as white patches to either side of the Dyke. In the foreground the Dyke turns sharply to the west.

number of large loops, notably between Martin and Timberland. The succeeding short stretch to the Slea is less tortuous. A length of that river to the south of North Kyme was fairly certainly canalised by the Roman engineers, and this adjustment of the natural watercourse led into a straight stretch of the canal, 4.8 km. in length. The Dyke then swings away to the south-east on another straight line across Heckington and Helpringham Fens. This length is well preserved and in a few places both the ditch and its banks form a still impressive monument. A number of straight lengths bring the canal to its crossing of the River Glen near Baston, and this point-to-point course continues south of the river as far as Market Deeping. From here to Eye, the line is again sinuous, there being two great loops at Peakirk and another at Eye, where, however, the engineers have decided to minimize the loop by cutting through a low ridge rather than go round it. This cutting is still clearly visible. The sector from the Welland to Eye contains some of the most impressive surviving lengths of the Car Dyke. South of Newark, however, it has suffered severely and its juncture with the Cat's Water and the Nene is obscured.[8]

Of the subsidiary lengths of artificial waterway which link with the Dyke there is little to report. Those for which a Roman origin seems likely are marked on the map (fig. 8). The more important of these are the Bourne — Morton canal, the two channels running across Rippingale Fen, Bourne Ea and the canalised courses of the Glen and Welland.[9]

The question whether there were associated with the Dyke such works as control- or check-points cannot yet be answered. No military works of any description are known for certain close to the canal, although one possible site deserves mention. This is a rectangular work with rounded corners at North Kyme.[10] It has now vanished, but it existed as a visible earthwork until at least 1870.

It is generally assumed that the course of the canal from Witham to Nene was cut at the same time as the artificial channels of the southern Fens, notably the Cambridgeshire Car Dyke. There is no basis in fact for believing that the two systems originated *at the same time*, although it is a reasonable hypothesis that at some time they were in simultaneous operation. Since no part of the Lincolnshire Dyke has yet been examined, no acceptable evidence for its date within the Roman period is available,[11] and it is probably unwise at this stage to give it the same date as the Cambridgeshire canal. In any case, the date of the latter is not securely fixed, the origin in the reign of Nero and the abandonment by the early third century suggested by Professor Clark being inadequately supported by the excavated pottery.[12] It is possible to speculate for a moment about the date of the Lincolnshire Dyke. It can hardly have come into existence before the draining of the Fens had begun, and the first organized works of reclamation now appear to belong to the reign of Hadrian (A.D. 117-38).[13] The construction of a major artery of trade and supply would find a probable historical context in that administration.

It is also commonly assumed that the entire course of the Car Dyke from Witham to Nene was laid out as a single entity at the same time. This is possible, but the different treatment accorded to different sectors should be noted. In the central and southern stretches there are long, straight sectors with only occasional bends and loops. In the northern sector, from the Witham to Metheringham, the work follows the contour at the very edge of the Fen and in doing so adopts a markedly sinuous course. There is no apparent reason for this difference in treatment, unless the Witham Fens to the east of this stretch had not yet been fully drained when the Dyke was dug, thus compelling the engineers to seek dryer land. The answer may lie in a difference of date, or in the methods adopted by different surveyors, or in both. Dogma is out of place on this subject before the spade has done its work.

In this account it has been assumed that the Car Dyke was designed from the outset as a canal. About a work of its length, dimensions and planning, no other conclusion appears reasonable. It may also, as Stukeley and several later writers[14] have suggested, have played a role in Fen drainage, by diverting water from the eastward-flowing streams, but this was an ancillary function only. Its prime purpose was to facilitate the movement of goods and commodities in bulk. What is now required is a full study of its history and of the local economy with which its existence was intimately bound up.

We should also briefly mention here the Raw Dykes at Leicester. This earthwork[15] has dimensions which are similar to the other canals in eastern Britain, its ditch being some 16.8 metres wide (fig. 10). Originally it reached to the southern fringes of the Roman city, but now only a length of 100 m. survives, about 2 km. from the south defences. The course of the remaining fragment is parallel to the River Soar. If this was indeed a canal, and its profile agrees with this idea, it is not clear what function it was designed to perform.[16] Nor is its Roman date established beyond doubt.

The tribal capital[17]

An examination of the Coritanian *chef-lieu* can best begin by discussing its Iron Age origins. There has long been dispute as to whether the site of Leicester (*Ratae Coritanorum*) was occupied before A.D. 43. The material published by Dr Kenyon in 1948[18] includes nothing that is certainly earlier than the time of the Roman conquest, but since the publication of her report rather more of the earliest levels beneath the Roman town have been available for examination and recent finds from these levels have produced concrete evidence that Leicester was indeed an Iron Age settlement.[19] The meagre total of Iron Age objects recovered so far, however, does not permit any assessment of its size and relative importance. The finds in question are Iron Age C pottery vessels, including cordoned bowls and pedestal urns, and coins. They probably date in the main from the first four decades of the first century A.D., although the occasional presence of much earlier material is to be noted. Thus far, the finds of Iron Age material have been made within the Roman walls, near the Jewry Wall, at Everard's Brewery, in Bath Lane and Redcross Street, but pre-Roman *Ratae* may presumably have been an extensive and disarticulate scatter of huts without any focus. It is difficult at the time of writing to foresee any opportunity for large-scale examination of the Iron Age levels. For the time being it must suffice us that there *was* an Iron Age phase in the history of the place and, since its Roman successor was to become the administrative centre of the Coritani, the Iron Age settlement was probably quite important in local political geography.

The first Roman occupation of Leicester almost certainly took the form of a military post. A few specifically military objects have suggested for some time that this was so. All come from sites beneath the later town: a legionary belt-plate from Blackfriars Street, a *gladius* pommel from between High Street and an eagle-head terminal from Royal Arcade.[20] An important clue to the whereabouts of the presumed fort is a short length of defensive ditch 1.83 m. wide and 91.5 cm. deep, with a V-shaped profile and a cleaning-channel, found in 1967 close to the present bank of the River Soar about 230 m. south-west of the Jewry Wall.[21] Apart from the profile of this ditch, commonly found in military works of the early Empire, pre-Flavian pottery from its filling points to an early date and thus most probably to a military origin. Its alignment is notably different from the later Roman streets but approximates closely with the line of the Fosse Way as this road approaches from the south-west. On the northern side of the town rectangular timber buildings of early Roman date have been recorded beneath the town defences[22] and, although the complete plan of these could not be recovered, their construction was in accord with military practice. If they were indeed buildings inside a fort, their alignment is such that they are unlikely to belong to the same work as the length of ditch. As on many other fort-sites in southern Britain, military occupation may well have entailed a succession of works of differing sizes on different alignments. A much earlier find from Leicester which may be connected with the invasion period is the tile from Black-friars bearing the retrograde stamp L VIII – Legio VIII.[23] This legion, or probably only a part of it, played a brief role in the invasion of Britain and had left the island by 44. It is difficult to explain the presence of this tile, unless it came to *Ratae* later in the Roman period. The legions in Britain did not begin to produce stamped tiles until they were established in more or less permanent quarters.

The military garrison is unlikely to have remained at Leicester for long after 70. About this time or shortly afterwards the *civitas Coritanorum* will have become an independent administrative unit. These formative years of civilian *Ratae*, the Flavian period and the early second century, have left very few intelligible traces of themselves. We should expect the first moves towards urban planning to have been taken now, and there are a few hints that this was so. The great public buildings, however, belong to a later time. These may be discussed first, before a perusal of the street-plan and the defences.

At first believed to be located on the Jewry Wall site,[24] the forum is now known to occupy *Insula* XXII, immediately east of the public baths.[25] A complete plan of the forum and its associated buildings will probably never be obtained, and it is only through excavation, and excavation of the most arduous kind, that the plan on fig. 11 can be offered. Limited space for excavation was not the only problem: the complex had been heavily robbed of its stone. The central courtyard was surrounded on its south, east and west sides by narrow ranges of rooms with porticoes facing in towards the court and out towards the street. The basilica appears to have lain on the northern side. Part at least of the west range had been partitioned into a series of small chambers, possibly long after the initial erection of the forum. These may have served some administrative function but they may with equal probability be identified as shops, nestling against the public building as so often in Roman monumental architecture. The work of erecting the forum began about 120, but there are signs of a later building-phase, probably set in motion before the completion of the original plan. It may be, then, that the ultimate form of the structure was not attained until the decade 130-40.[26]

A substantial part of *Insula* XVI, north of the forum (fig. 12), was occupied by a large public building, one element in which was a basilican hall, running in all probability across the entire width of the *insula*.[27] This structure overlay the remains of the fine early second century dwelling described below, and was built between about 180 and 200. The most striking feature of the building, as it is at present known, is the great hall, 11.3 m. in width and with flanking aisles to north and south giving further widths of 5.25 and 4.95 m. respectively. Its length was probably more than 46 m. Northward of the north aisle, the building appears

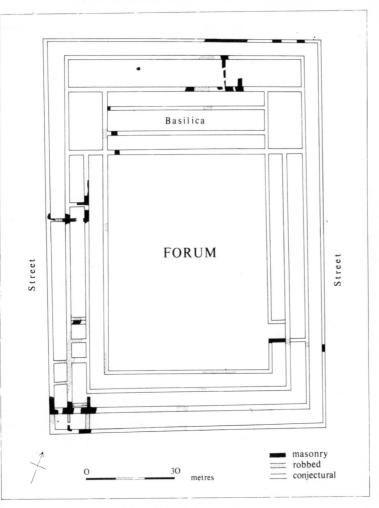

Basilica

FORUM

Street

Street

	masonry
	robbed
	conjectural

O   30
                    metres

11. Plan of the Leicester Forum

to have been partitioned into narrower ranges, each measuring about 3.05 m. wide. Much of the rest of the *insula* lies
beneath modern streets and there is little hope of recovering
more of the plan of this unusual structure in the
near future. Excavation produced no clue to its function, but
plainly the great hall was designed to accommodate a
concourse of people and the siting close to the commercial

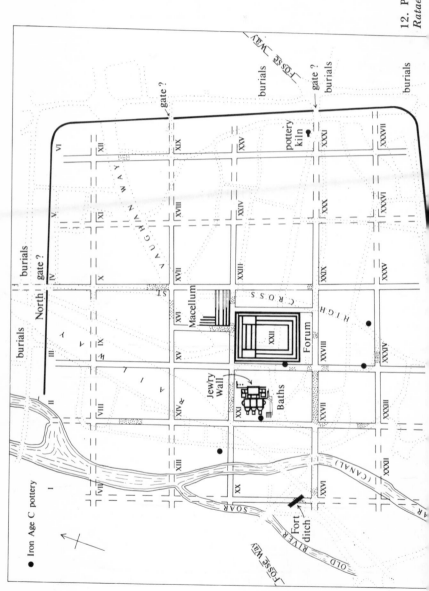

12. Plan of *Ratae Coritanorum*

centre of the town suggests a connection with trade. A market-hall or *macellum* is the most plausible identification, possibly used by several tradesmen with interests in a particular field. Several Roman towns had more than one market-place (Cologne is the best documented case)[28] and in such cases the various markets may have had specialised functions or dealt in particular commodities. Much earlier discoveries of good quality mouldings and part of a cornice at the junction of Blue Boar Lane and High Cross Street are probably to be related to the *macellum* or to some other monumental structure at the heart of the town.

Leicester's only fragment of a Roman building surviving above ground, the Jewry Wall, has long excited speculation. During the eighteenth and nineteenth centuries an identification as the west gate of the town found favour from time to time and it was not until Dr Kenyon's excavations of 1936-9 that its structural role as part of a monumental building complex was finally revealed.[29] Haverfield had in 1918, with his customary acumen, linked the Jewry Wall with the public baths of *Ratae*, and so it turned out.

The complex comprises a large basilican hall, the *palaestra* or exercise-hall, and to the west of this the baths themselves (fig. 13). The Jewry Wall is all that remains of the west wall of the basilica, dividing it from the baths. Two large entrances are still visible in the Jewry Wall, allowing passage between the baths and the *palaestra*. Of the latter little could be excavated, since it lies beneath St. Nicholas' church and churchyard. The plan of the baths, however, has been almost completely revealed. They were not elaborately planned, even by the modest standards of Roman Britain. The essence of their layout is symmetry about an east-west axis, a form of planning which is a mark of the Hadrianic baths at Leptis Magna. On leaving the *palaestra* for the baths, the bather passed through one of the great entrances into a large room or court.[30] To either side of this lay a group of three small chambers, each group bounded by an L-shaped corridor. These rooms were for cold bathing (*frigidaria*) and may have included cold plunge-baths. There followed a row of somewhat larger rooms offering warmer baths (*tepidaria*) and then on the west side of the complex there lay a still larger range

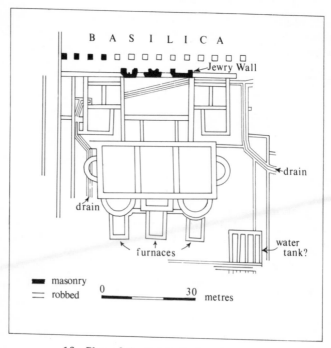

13. Plan of the Public Baths of Leicester

of rooms, for hot bathing (*caldaria*). This range was divided into three rooms of roughly equal size: overall it measured 36.6 by 18.3 m. The end rooms had large semicircular apses in their west sides, and the central chamber was furnished with a rectangular recess on the same side. These will have housed the hot plunge-baths or perhaps sweat-baths (*laconica*). Outside each of these projections lay a furnace. Smaller apses were also provided in the shorter sides of the range.

The whole building had been too heavily robbed for the system of water-supply to be fully recovered or understood, but at least some of the outfall drains were located. These can still be traced on the site and they appear on the plan (fig. 13). Dr Kenyon argued that the series of close-set walls at the south-west corner of the site had supported a reservoir or tank and that this was the main water-supply for the baths. This is a real possibility, but it is impossible at present to see how the water was distributed to the appropriate parts of the building.

The cumulative evidence for the date of erection of the baths points to the period shortly after A.D. 150.

The dating of the town defences has already been commented on (above, p. 36) and it has been observed that there is as yet no ground for dating their erection before the third century. Precisely when they went up can only be determined by the collection of more dating evidence and by more work on the chronology of third-century pottery, a long-standing stumbling block. The lines of the north, south and east sides have been fairly closely defined: the minimum area which can have been contained by them is 45.3 ha. (fig. 12). The wall measured some 2.74 m. at its base and fronted an earth rampart with which it was contemporary. The fullest evidence for the ditch-system to date comes from the south side. Near the wall lay a ditch 6.1 m. wide and 2.44 m. deep. Further out and separated from this by a gap of .91 metres lay a larger ditch, 10.2 m. wide and 3.05 m. deep. This larger obstacle may have been added to the defensive system late in the Roman period. Both ditches lay open until the medieval period. In two places, dry-stone foundations have been observed projecting into the inner ditch, suggesting a strengthening of the wall-foundation, such as might have been made necessary by the addition of external towers. The evidence for this, however, is not cogent.[31]

The western side of the defences, towards the Soar, has so far defied attempts to locate it. All trace of the medieval defences also on this side has vanished, clear proof that the river has played the major role in the disappearance of both defensive works. Since the river and the canal occupy so much ground and since the rest of the area is heavily built up, only a lucky chance seems likely to reveal where the west defences of *Ratae* lay. Two clues are to hand, neither however of much worth. First, a Roman north-south street is known on the land between the Soar and the canal, more than 229 m. west of the Jewry Wall.[32] This might appear to suggest that the west wall should be sought *west* of the present course of the river, but it should not be forgotten that at several Romano-British towns the defences enclose an area smaller than that covered by the earlier street-plan, and that therefore this street may have been excluded from the walled area. Secondly, since it is a reasonable inference that the Roman north gate lay beneath, or close to, its medieval successor, and if it were centrally placed in the northern side, the western defences should run a little to the west of Bath Lane along the east bank of the Soar and the canal. At some point in this street, a massive wall was recorded in the seventeenth century. The Romans, however, observed no rigid rules in the siting of their town gates. The only satisfactory arguments towards a solution of the problem will be based on further field-work.

The site of none of the gates is known for certain but the projected lines of certain streets permit speculation. Thus the known line of the main north-south street appears to fix the Roman north gate either beneath or in the near vicinity of that of the medieval period. The same street when projected to meet the south defences gives reason for placing the Roman south gate some way to the west of its medieval successor. The position of the east gate is more problematic. If, as seems most probable, the main Roman east-west street was that which ran past the south side of the forum (this being also the line of the main medieval east-west street), this would suggest that the Roman gate lay beneath that of the medieval period. As a working hypothesis this is here accepted. But it must be noted that this argument locates the gate only about a third of the way along the east side. Perhaps another gate or postern existed between the east gate and the north-east angle. The approaches of the Fosse Way to the east and west sides of the town are not clearly enough defined to throw any light on the matter. Indeed this subject raises problems of its own.[33] It cannot be assumed that the Roman road approached the town on precisely the same line as its medieval and modern successors.

The remains of lesser public buildings are not extensive. Excavations in St. Nicholas' Circle in 1969 revealed almost the entire plan of a large aisled building, the total length of which was slightly over 30.5 m.[34] At its west end lay a room some 12.2 m. long, the plan of which was too damaged for complete recovery. The main part of the structure was divided into nave and aisles, the nave floor being about 46 cm. lower than that of the aisles. The east end had transepts, their ends terminating in half-apses. The aisled plan and the fact that the nave is sunken tempt identification as a *mithraeum*, though no conclusive evidence as to its function is forthcoming. If it was indeed a *mithraeum*, it is of great interest, being only the second such temple to be recorded outside the military zone of the province and the largest of all the known instances in Britain. Its great size and the relative prominence of its siting, however, make one wonder whether it can have been a *mithraeum*. It would appear strange if Mithras had a sizeable following in *Ratae*, and even if he had, the siting of this building near to the town-centre does not seem appropriate to the temple of a mystery cult.

No certain sites of temples are known and relatively few pieces of religious sculpture have been recovered. From Blue Boar Lane comes a relief of a bearded and draped male god, evidently a water-deity.[35] This formed part of an altar or possibly a much larger relief. A statue-base found near the Jewry Wall bears the inscription.

MERC . . . . .
PROP . . . .

which may be expanded into MERCURIO PROPITIO. The upper part of this dedication has perished.[36]

With only few exceptions, the plans of private dwellings in the town are not very informative. No complete house-plans have yet been recovered. For the most part, all that it has been possible to record or salvage amounts to a number of mosaic floors (figs 14 & 15) and many incoherent fragments of buildings. Inevitably, it is the humbler dwellings which fail to receive due record. In Leicester, there is virtually nothing to be said about them. Fortunately, the succession of more pretentious buildings near Blue Boar Lane, as well as being the best recorded dwellings of *Ratae*, also reveal many points of intrinsic interest.[37]

The earliest house, of which little could be examined, was a timber structure erected in the Flavian period. Not long after 100, it was demolished and a house with stone foundations and clay and concrete floors took its place. The plan comprised a series of wings about a porticoed court. The superstructure of the walls was of unbaked bricks of clay set in a gravelly clay mixture, a form of construction which may have been commoner in Roman Britain than our records indicate. The individual bricks could be identified, their usual dimensions being 20.5-30.5 cm. by 38-43 by 5-10. Before about 150 the house was given a thorough renovation. Tessellated floors were inserted and the inner wall of the courtyard portico was replastered and painted in a formal, classical manner. Some at least of the scenes portrayed are shown in three dimensions, in a style which recalls Italian work of the first century A.D. This wall-painting is one of the most ambitious of surviving frescoes from Roman Britain, and may well attest the presence of an Italian or Gaulish artist in Antonine *Ratae*. Strangely, this splendid phase in the history of the house was shortly followed by dereliction and squalor. The roof was stripped off and the plaster tumbled from the walls. By about 180, the ruined structure was swept away, to be replaced by the market-hall already described (above, p. 56).

Another house of good quality lay in *Insula* XXVIII, off the modern Southgate Street.[38] All trace of the building above the Roman ground level seems to have been destroyed, but a remarkable cellar survived almost intact, an uncommon feature in a Romano-British town-house. The cellar measured some 3 metres square, its well-built granite walls surviving to a height of about 1.8 m. These had been plastered and painted white, with narrow red and blue bands running diagonally across the corners. In each wall was a recess, 91 cm. high, 91 cm. wide and 30.5 cm. deep, and two of the walls had in addition sloping window embrasures some 91 cm. wide.

For the rest, the plans of domestic buildings are poorly recorded. The evidence of an important series of mosaic floors, however, indicates that several other private houses may been the peers of that in Blue Boar Lane in the quality of their interior decoration. One of the finest of all Romano-British geometric mosaics is that from Blackfriars,[39] now preserved *in situ* beneath part of Leicester railway station (fig. 14). This floor takes the form of a nine-octagon

14. The Blackfriars mosaic, Leicester

grid, each octagon containing roundels decorated in very fine detail. The four corner roundels have been executed with outstanding skill, to give a brilliant impression of rapid motion. Another outstanding pavement comes from a house in St. Nicholas Street.[40] This too consists of a nine-octagon grid, and eight of the octagons are treated in a purely geometric way. In the central panel, however, the artist has placed a peacock (fig. 15) which is viewed from the front: the motif is nowhere else recorded in Britain.[41] Both the Blackfriars and the so-called Peacock pavements probably belong to the second half of the second century, a time which clearly saw rapid progress both in the erection of public buildings and in the larger private residences. The later pavements so far recorded are of poorer quality. One found in the late seventeenth century near All Saints Church[42] shows Cyparissus and his pet stag, a scene otherwise unrecorded on Romano-British mosaics. This floor reveals considerable ambition in the craftsman who laid it, an ambition unfortunately not matched by his craftsmanship.

It will be obvious from what has been said about the circumstances of discovery and excavation in the town that little can yet be said about the life and livelihood of the inhabitants of *Ratae*. No large-scale industry is known to have been carried on. Like medieval and Tudor Leicester, trades and services associated with agriculture would have supplied most of the city's artisans with work. No doubt a wide range of crafts was pursued, but likely traces of only two have been recorded: pottery-making and perhaps leather-manufacture.[43] The leisure-time pursuits of the citizenry can only be conjured up by analogy. It is by no means surprising that the sole piece of evidence for their amusements mentions a dancer and a gladiator. This fragment, a graffito on a samian sherd,[44] does not by itself prove the existence of an amphitheatre at Leicester, although a city of this size and evident wealth might well have boasted one.

The immediate surroundings of the Roman town have naturally been more haphazardly recorded than the interior. Cremation burials have been found outside the walls on the north, south and east sides, and at a few points within the walls also: e.g., St. Martin's Lane, the Market Place, High Street and a site west of the Jewry Wall. These clearly must date from before the erection of the defences. Later inhumation graves have been recorded outside all four sides, the latest of all being those beyond the south wall, in Millstone Lane and Newarke Street.

Known buildings in the suburbs are few indeed. The most striking is a fairly large villa of courtyard plan at Norfolk Street, earlier termed the Cherry Orchard or Danett's Hall villa.[45] This lies 1½ km. west of the town. Part of one wing and its mosaic floors, together with the corridor of another range, was explored in 1782 and again in the following century. A date in the fourth century is probable for the mosaics, but since the site of the house is now built over there is no immediate hope of unravelling its history.

15. Central panel of the Peacock mosaic, Leicester

Minor urban settlements

An important group of settlements which have too rarely
figured in discussions about the Romano-British countryside
is the varied class of site which includes road-side settlements
of varying size and pretension and other nucleated settlements.[46] We must beware of generalising about these
settlements since so few have been satisfactorily examined.
The structural history of the defences of a few has been

carefully elucidated, but the all-important information about their lay-out, development and economy is just beginning to accumulate. It is, however, fairly clear that the majority of them had the closest links with the surrounding countryside and that they performed many of the functions of agricultural villages. Those which received defences have attracted more attention than the others, but it must not be thought that the undefended villages were necessarily different in character or less deserving of study.

The most extensive excavation of a road-side *vicus* as yet has been carried through at *Margidunum*.[47] Here, buildings of simple plan straggle along both margins of the Fosse Way for more than half a mile, the great majority lying close to the frontage itself. Several buildings are rectangular blocks without many subdivisions, this being the commonest house-type in 'small towns'. One or two dwellings were more elaborate: for example, a three-roomed block with its long axis parallel with the main road and set back a few yards from it. Another was a small portico-house of the fourth century, resembling a small villa. None of the excavated dwellings appear to be much earlier than about 150 and several are much later. A remarkable feature of the plan of this site is the amount of space within the defences which was never built over. Few buildings are known away from the main frontage, a situation known at many other road-side settlements. Since the depth of soil here is relatively slight, however, it is possible that many insubstantial timber structures have either been completely obliterated by the plough or have eluded detection in the black peaty soil which masks the Roman levels. Many agricultural sites, including two villas and another settlement, have been recorded within a radius of five miles of *Margidunum* and it is clear that a considerable agricultural population was nucleated upon this village. It is from road-side settlements like *Margidunum* that the colonisation of new land was advanced in the first century of the Roman occupation. A detailed study of this fragment of the Coritanian countryside would be extremely informative.

One of the first 'small towns' of Roman Britain to be subjected to study is that which grew out of the *canabae* of the early auxiliary fort at Great Casterton.[48] The area of settlement enclosed by defences in the third century is about 7 hectares, but Roman buildings may remain undetected outside the line of the wall, especially along Ermine Street. Within the walls only one building has been fully excavated, this being a small block 11.6 m. by 6.7 m. This may have been an outbuilding to a larger structure rather than a dwelling. Elsewhere within the defences, the excavators found that, as at *Margidunum*, considerable areas had never been built over and that a street-plan had not developed.[49]

What is known about the other settlements indicates that they all had a straggling lay-out without any focus. Planning was elementary, a few streets branching off from the main road, as at Brough. Buildings too were simple, normally rectangular blocks with few or no subdivisions. Aisled houses put in an occasional appearance, as at Ancaster and Old Sleaford.[50] At one site, Dragonby, some dwellings had rounded ends, thus resembling certain buildings on peasant sites in the Fens and in Northumberland.[51] Some settlements have been only recently discovered, for instance Navenby, half way between Lincoln and Ancaster, and Foston.[52] Others may yet emerge. Presumably many of them served as market centres for the surrounding countryside, and were thus logical developments from a Roman system of land-owning. In several cases, however, it seems likely that they were not independent settlements, but rather were associated with large agricultural units, notably villa-estates. This is the most rational explanation of the close juxtaposition of individual villas with several nucleated settlements. The more striking cases are Sapperton and the Haceby villa, High Cross and Sapcote, Hibaldstow and the Sturton villa, and possibly Dragonby and Winterton. Regrettably, even after total excavation, such an association is unlikely to be proved, but this is one possible explanation of where the *coloni* of late Roman estates resided: in nucleated villages away from the villas themselves.

4.

Rural settlement

Like England until long after 1700, Roman Britain was substantially a land of farmers and peasants. The life and work of the province Britannia was life on the land. Almost all the Coritani were closely connected with the life of the countryside, as landlords, as tenants or *coloni* on estates, or as peasant freeholders. Unfortunately, the importance of the subject is not matched by the quality of the available evidence. This is not entirely the fault of those who have worked in this field. The blame can fairly be put upon the evidence itself, for there are many aspects of rural affairs that purely archaeological evidence, by its very nature, can never illumine. The tenurial problems are particularly tantalizing, but there are many others. The sizes of villa-estates and lesser farms, the proportions of slaves to free peasants on large estates, the relation of peasant or 'native' settlements to villas, the different crop-yields in different areas, the variations in profitability of different crops at different times — on all these major subjects we cannot be hopeful of improving on our almost total ignorance. While admitting all this, however, there is still much to be evaluated and to whet the appetite for the results of further research.

It will be borne in mind that the fabric of Celtic society survived the Roman conquest essentially intact and that this society was a complex weave of the relationships of men to their masters. This was more naturally characteristic of rural than of urban societies, more appropriate to clusters of families than to large communities. The peasant of pre-Roman Britain was bound by obligations of service to his master, the noble to his chief, the chief to the tribal or provincial king. It can be reasonably assumed that the Romano-British peasantry, *mutatis mutandis*, continued to owe obligations to landowners, and therefore that peasant settlements were often not isolated and independent units, but were linked to the domains of men of higher degree by bonds which leave no archaeological trace. It is doubtful whether it will ever be possible to discern clearly such relationships, but it should never be forgotten that they existed. Another thing which must not be overlooked is the close connexion between towns and the countryside in the Roman Empire. Although we possess no specific information about the pattern of land-ownership among the Coritani, it is probable that it was complex. In antiquity land was the safest and most desirable investment for anyone with money to spare. Thus, businessmen or craftsmen living in *Ratae* or *Lindum* could purchase land far from those cities and let it to a tenant farmer. Further, large estates need not be single blocks of land. They were not infrequently made up of small parcels of land scattered over a wide area. This is yet another aspect of rural affairs that archaeological evidence cannot reveal to us.

It is essential that we begin our discussion with the natural environment, since this controls the development of rural settlement in any period. In particular the production of food was determined in large measure by the soil-types of the region. Broadly speaking, the early settler encountered three main kinds of soil in the east Midlands: the alluvium and gravel of the river valleys, the light soils of the oolite and sandstone uplands, and the heavy clays south of the Trent (fig. 16). The light soils produced by the river gravels require no further comment, their perennial attractiveness for pre-historic and later settlement being fully documented else-where.[1] Other light and workable soils were to be found on the limestones of the Jurassic ridge. These are represented by a wide range of types with many local variants. All, however, are characterised by their lightness and most could have supported both arable and mixed farming. The heavy claylands are still something of an unknown factor in agricultural settlement. They have for long been dismissed as forested wastes in the Roman period, defying settlement until the Saxon or medieval clearance. It is becoming clearer that this generalisation is far too sweeping. Several areas of the claylands do indeed appear to have been thinly settled in the Roman period, while others were already being freely exploited.[2]

It must be realized that this picture of the regional soils is a gross simplification. In actuality, the soil-types are extremely varied, so much so that the extent of the individual variants are still being mapped. So as to provide a more meaningful background to the Roman pattern of settlement, the tribal territory is divided into regions on the basis of the *prevalent* soil-types.[3] This makes no allowance for local variations, but at least forms a framework within which the relative density of settlement can be estimated (fig. 16).

Away from the densely settled alluvium of the Trent, Soar, Wreak and Welland, the most extensive areas of light, easily worked land lie on the limestone uplands of Lincolnshire, Rutland and Northamptonshire. We would expect to find more settlements on this land than we do. The truth is probably that the settlements themselves lay mainly on the lower slopes, except where water was available from springs on the scarp. A few important villas, however, are found on the Lincolnshire ridge: Roxby, Scampton and Haceby. In the central sector of the ridge, there is a remarkable nucleation of agricultural settlements on the light sandy soil of the Ancaster Gap, about the small town of Ancaster (above, p. 38). Not all areas of light soil, however, are so benign. The distinctive undulating landscape created by the Bunter Sandstone is still today largely occupied by the heaths and thickets of Sherwood Forest and the Dukeries. This land is more suited to the training of tank crews than to agriculture. The soil is a light sandy loam, highly porous and thus subject to drought. In dry weather extensive sand-blows occur, stripping away the topmost inch of the field-surface. There is little sign that any part of this area attracted prehistoric or Roman settlement. Only in the little valleys of the Meden, Maun and Poulter are a few Roman sites recorded, and it was here too that early medieval land colonisation began.

Areas of mixed soil conditions are the Chalk Wolds of

Lincolnshire and the sands and clays of north Lindsey. Away from the valley alluvium, the latter area is characterised by large areas of blown sand. Roman settlement was fairly dense and included several large villas. By contrast, early medieval settlement was thin and scattered. The surface of the Wolds is not uniformly of chalk. In the south, the many small tributaries of the river Steeping have cut through the chalk to reveal sandstone and clay, and in numerous places elsewhere the chalk is masked by Boulder Clay and gravel. The chalk itself produces a shallow but fairly rewarding soil and several nucleated settlements occur on it. The known villas, however, lie close to the margins of the Lindsey Clay Vale. The limestone country of west Nottinghamshire also has varied soils. The Coal Measures normally produce a stiff clay, difficult to work without extensive drainage. The Magnesian limestone by contrast yields a light loam, easy to work, well drained, and thus admirably suited to arable farming.[4]

Most of the remaining regions on our map are areas of heavy soil. Several are today among the most fertile areas of the Midlands. The most important are as follows.

Lindsey Clay Vale and the Clay Wolds

Although there are large patches of blown sand at the northern end, this region is one of glacial gravel and Boulder Clay. It is possible that there were tracts of woodland here in the Roman period, as there were in the eleventh century A.D.

Kesteven Claylands

This is fertile, heavy land on the Fen margins. A fair number of Roman sites occur on it but villas are few. It may have carried a considerable amount of woodland in antiquity as it does today.

Keuper Marl Plateau of Nottinghamshire

Roman sites are abundant on this excellent land, and this is plainly one region of heavy soil which did not deter colonisation. Surprisingly few villas have yet been recorded.

Vale of Belvoir and the Wolds of Notts. and Leics.
These are regions of Lias Clay, with excellent soils long famous for pastoral farming. The Vale of Belvoir, in particular, is beginning to reveal a dense Roman settlement, foreshadowing that revealed by the Domesday Survey.[5]

West Leics. Uplands
This is a region of variable soils, produced by Keuper Marl and Boulder Clay — the kind of terrain which may well have been wooded in antiquity as it was in the early middle ages. Present evidence suggests that Roman settlement was sparse.

East Leics. Uplands and the Vale of Catmose
Another region of varied soils, the best of them being derived from the Marlstones. Boulder Clay covers much of the area and hence some tracts have heavy soils. Settlement seems to have been fairly evenly distributed, though the detailed picture has yet to be worked out. The recorded villas lie in the Vale of Catmose rather than further west.

Lutterworth Uplands
This Boulder Clay region was probably difficult to cultivate in antiquity. Along its northern edge, however, the soils are derived from the Oolite and the Upper Lias and thus offer a more tractable environment.

Rockingham Forest
Although densely wooded in medieval and later times, this region of Boulder Clay was widely settled in the Roman period. Several villas lay at its south-western end, including Great Weldon, Oakley and Stanion.

Finally, there are a few regions of individual character, none of them immediately attractive to settlement. The Isle of Axholme and the Carrs of north Nottinghamshire seem not to have been systematically drained in the Roman period and, although a few settlements are known, colonisation here was very limited until the seventeenth century reclamation. The coastal marshland of Lincolnshire also did not share in

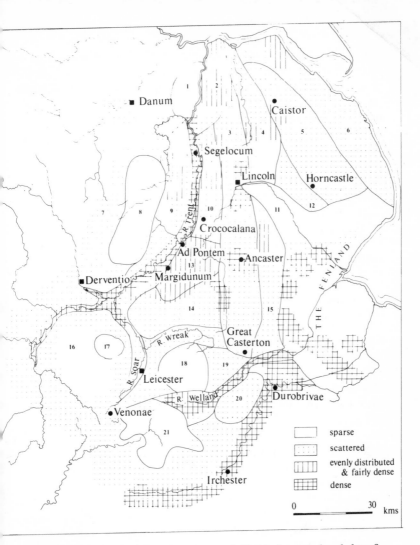

1. Isle of Axholme and the N. Notts. Carrs 2. N. Lindsey sand and clays 3. Lincs, limestone uplands 4. Lindsey clay vale 5. Chalk Wolds 6. Lincs. coastal marshland 7. Magnesian limestone 8. Sherwood Forest (Bunter sandstone) 9. Keuper Marl of E. Notts. 10. Trent Valley clay lowlands 11. Witham peat fens 12. Clay Wolds 13. Vale of Belvoir (Boulder Clay) 14. Notts. & Leics. Wolds (Boulder Clay) 15. Kesteven claylands 16. W. Leics. uplands 17. Charnwood Forest 18. E. Leics uplands 19. Vale of Catmose 20. Rockingham Forest 21. Lutterworth uplands

16. Generalised distribution of agricultural settlement in the later Roman period

the systematic drainage accorded to the Fens, but settlement of a humble kind was possible. Villas and villages are unknown here. No Roman settlements have been recorded in the Witham fens and they too clearly had no part in the great drainage programme of the second century A.D.[6] Only a few, scattered settlements are known on the old igneous rocks of Charnwood Forest, an infertile area which is still thinly settled.

The pattern of Roman settlement can as yet be mapped only in the most generalised terms (fig. 16). The map may be taken to represent the distribution of agricultural settlement in the period A.D. 250-350. It is not yet possible to reveal changes in the settlement pattern during all four Roman centuries.

The villas

One of the most serious gaps in our knowledge of the *civitas Coritanorum* is the appalling lack of information about many aspects of the villas. The architecture and planning of some villas, it is true, have been thoroughly studied in the past,[7] so thoroughly that this aspect needs no extensive treatment here. But the less tangible social and economic aspects still offer a considerable field of research. Out of some sixty known Coritanian villas, hardly one has yet been fully and satisfactorily examined with the necessary expertise and with an understanding of what these sites can be made to reveal.[8] The materials, then, for a general account of the villas have not yet been gathered, and the best we can do is to discuss the evidence provided by certain villas which are representative of various levels of wealth and social degree, choosing sites which have been recently examined. It is not our aim to provide a detailed account of any single villa. For these, the reader must turn to the excavation reports.

Bearing in mind the large area covered by the tribe, villas are far from numerous in the region. When the total number, about 60 at present, is compared with that recorded for other lowland tribes, the Coritani make a poor showing. There is also a striking rarity of large and well-appointed residences such as could compare with those of the Dobunni or the

Regnenses. Only three large villas are recorded, and one of these, Norfolk Street, lay within the suburbs of *Ratae*. The other two are the houses at Southwell (Notts.) and Scampton (Lincs.).[9] Even large portico-houses are relatively rare. The great majority of the Romanised farms are very simple, having at their centres small portico villas or, much more commonly, aisled halls. This commonest class of villa plainly does not represent the homes of the wealthy landed Coritani. More probably, they represent either the homes of moderately prosperous peasants who have in course of time attained a higher living standard or they are subsidiary units in a large estate, each unit being run by a bailiff or tenant-farmer.

A crude classification of the better known villas can be achieved by dividing them into three classes. Class I contains the villas which might bear comparison with the largest of the entire province, the courtyard houses of Bignor, North Leigh and Woodchester, although none of the Coritanian instances appear to be as large as these. Class II is made up of those houses which, in their ultimate form, consisted of portico-houses, often with an ancillary aisled hall or halls. Class III includes the humbler farms, mainly small portico-houses and isolated aisled halls. This classification is naturally subject to many limiting factors: the condition of the surviving remains, the quality of the excavation which revealed them, and not least the tastes of the Roman occupiers.

Using these criteria, the following classification of Coritanian villas is suggested.

CLASS I	CLASS II	CLASS III
Norfolk St.	Barnack?	Ancaster
Scampton	Great Casterton	Ashley
Southwell	Great Weldon	Barholm
	Greetwell?	Barton in Fabis
	Haceby	Car Colston
	Helpston?	Cottingham
	Horkstow	Cromwell
	Mansfield Woodhouse	Denton
	Medbourne?	Empingham

Norton Disney	Epperstone
Oldcotes	Lockington
Roxby	Maxey
Rothley?	Oakley
Sapcote?	Shirebrook
Stoke Rochford	Stanion
Thistleton Dyer	Thurgarton
Winterton	Tickencote
	Walesby
	Weekley
	Worlaby

At least twenty other sites are known, which excavation will probably prove to be villas. Of these, the greater number is likely to belong to Class III. Some of the Class II villas may in reality be larger than they at present appear. The Great Casterton villa, for instance, may well be only partially known as yet, the main dwelling-house lying to the east of the excavated buildings. Several other sites in this group, for example, Horkstow, Roxby, Greetwell, Oldcotes and Stoke Rochford were examined long ago and their plans are sketchily recorded.

A look at the map (fig. 17) makes it clear that the known villas are not uniformly distributed over all the region. Few have been recorded on the alluvium of the Trent, Soar and Wreak. Only two or three sites of villas lie on the Trent gravels (Cromwell, Lockington and perhaps Shardlow). Otherwise peasant farms without any recognizeable *foci* predominate. This picture cannot be the result of an imbalance in fieldwork, for the Trent valley has been subjected to a considerable amount of systematic study, from the air in particular. On the Welland gravels, by contrast, notably in the Stamford region, a number of simple villas have been recorded: Barnack, Barholm and Helpston. Several areas show no villas at all, and in some of these cases it is almost certain that the map reflects the true state of affairs in Roman times. The coastal marshland of Lincolnshire and the Fenland are cases in point. The light soil of Sherwood Forest is another. The heavy clays in the southern parts of the canton, the west Leics. uplands, the east Leics. heights and

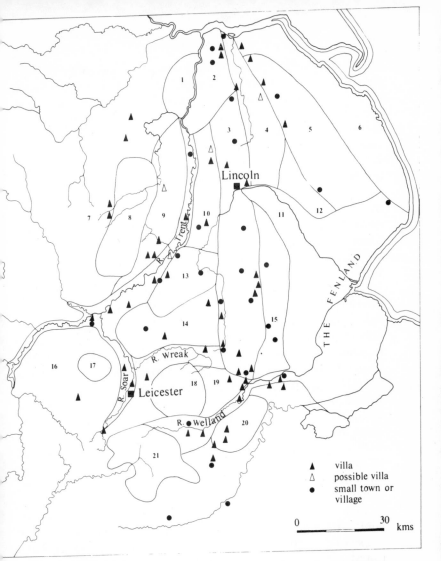

1. Isle of Axholme and the N. Notts. Carrs 2. N. Lindsey sands and clays 3. Lincs. limestone uplands 4. Lindsey clay vale 5. Chalk Wolds 6. Lincs. coastal marshland 7. Magnesian limestone 8. Sherwood Forest (Bunter sandstone) 9. Keuper Marl of E. Notts. 10. Trent Valley clay lowlands 11. Witham peat fens 12. Clay Wolds 13. Vale of Belvoir (Boulder Clay) 14. Notts. & Leics. Wolds (Boulder Clay) 15. Kesteven claylands 16. W. Leics. uplands 17. Charnwood Forest 18. E. Leics uplands 19. Vale of Catmose 20. Rockingham Forest 21. Lutterworth uplands

17. Distribution of villas and 'small towns'

the Lutterworth uplands can show very few villas as yet, although these are areas where fieldwork has not yet been intensive. In Lincolnshire, the clay Wolds and the Kesteven clays have yet to produce a single villa. By and large, then, the heavy claylands appear to have supported few villa-estates. A glance at the other areas of Boulder Clay and Keuper Marl (Keuper Marl of east Notts., Vale of Belvoir and the Notts. and Leics. Wolds) confirms this, although again we must stress the inchoate nature of fieldwork. Surprisingly, the Boulder Clay of Rockingham Forest supported several villas, including the large house at Great Weldon. In general terms, however, this region can provide little support for the argument that villa owners began to exploit the heavier clayland in the middle and later Roman period.

The great majority of the villas lie on the light and intermediate soils produced by the loam terrains, the limestone of Lincolnshire and the Lindsey sands. A considerable number lie on the limestone of central and south Lincolnshire, especially between the Ancaster Gap and the Welland. The sands and clays of north Lindsey also have a notable group of prosperous villas, including Roxby, Horkstow and Winterton. The western edge of the Chalk Wolds is dotted with rather small villas, sited along the spring-line. On the eastern slopes, they are as yet unknown.

It is difficult to discern marked local concentrations of villas. An interesting group appears to centre on Great Casterton, another on the light sandy soil about Ancaster. Others lie still closer to small towns and roadside villages, e.g. Brough-*Crococalana*, Thorpe-*Ad Pontem* and *Margidunum*, while the Lockington villa may have had a peasant village associated with it (below, p. 98). As has frequently been noted in the case of the other Romano-British civitates, relatively few villas lie within a radius of 20-25 km. from the walls of the major towns. This is strikingly true in the case of Lincoln. In the environs of the city, only Scampton and Greetwell lay within easy reach of *Lindum*. Even the desirable limestone country to north and south has not yet produced any certain villas within about 30 km. of the city. A few villas are known within a similar radius of the walls of Leicester, although, as has been already noted, they are apparently unknown on the heavy land to the east and south of *Ratae*. In both cases, the land close to the cities was presumably farmed by landowners who were domiciled within the walls.

Turning now to the villas themselves, representatives of these three classes may be examined.

CLASS I

Southwell

This is probably the largest villa yet discovered among the Coritani. The details of its plan so far recovered suggest that at the peak of its development the house consisted of an arrangement of wings round a central courtyard. One range contained mosaics in mid- or late- fourth-century styles, matched at other Coritanian villas, notably Horkstow, Denton and Haceby.[10] Another wing contained a bath-suite, of which a large cold plunge bath could be excavated. The upper parts of the walls of this bath had been decorated with richly painted scenes, including animal and human figures, fish, and flowers.[11] The building so far revealed was certainly occupied in the fourth century, and probably no earlier. It had, however, replaced another dwelling of the later second century. No dateable material earlier than about 150 has been found on the site. Presumably the great fourth-century residence was the centre of an estate which covered most of the fertile little valley of the Greet.

Scampton (fig. 18)

A substantial part of the plan of a large villa was traced here in 1795, on a hill-top site close to, and west of, the junction of Till Bridge Lane and Ermine Street, five miles north of Lincoln. Naturally, hardly any of the associated finds were recorded, and the outline plan of the residence is the only result of the excavation to hold our attention. Three main ranges of rooms were disposed about a large oblong courtyard, or possibly two smaller courts. The courtyard was entered from a portico running the length of the west side. To the south and east lay the principal residential quarters, to

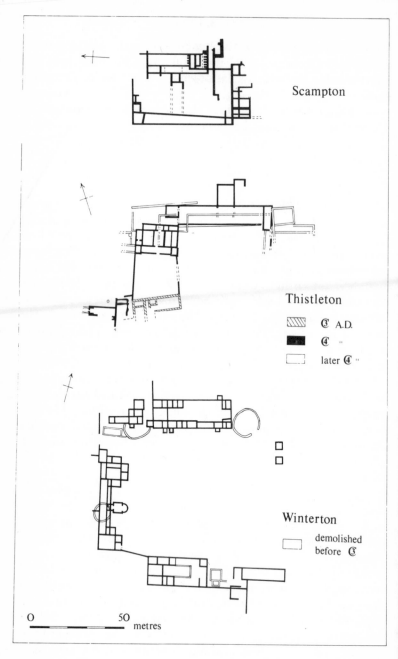

Scampton

Thistleton

▨ C A.D.

■ C "

☐ later C "

Winterton

☐ demolished
before C

0 ____ 50
metres

18. Plans of the villas at Scampton (Lincs.), Thistleton Dyer (Rutland),
and Winterton (Lincs.)

the north humbler buildings, which may have housed the domestic staff. The extent of all the main buildings was not ascertained, but from north to south the complex measured more than 46 m. and from east to west probably much more than 37 m. By analogy with the other courtyard villas of Britain, this lay-out presumably belongs to the fourth century. Nothing is otherwise known of the history of the building.[12]

CLASS II

Mansfield Woodhouse (Notts.)

The Mansfield Woodhouse villa, first excavated in 1786 and restudied in 1936-9,[13] is in a sense an outlier of the main system. Hardly any other villas are known in the west Nottinghamshire hills, or in the relatively broad and fertile valleys of the Derwent and the Wye. Within 8 km. to the north of Mansfield Woodhouse there are several peasant settlements of a pre-eminently Highland type.[14] But this villa is very far from being a primitive representative of its type. It will stand comparison in its domestic equipment with Winterton, or with Ditchley (Oxon.), and it must have contrasted sharply with the extreme rusticity of the surrounding hilly countryside. This contrast leads us to question whether the owner of the villa in its late Roman heyday had achieved his prosperous condition on his native heath, or whether he came from another part of the *civitas* or of the province. If the latter were the case, there is no doubt that he found the land already under cultivation. The earliest farm on the site was established about the end of the first century A.D. or early in the second. Its lay-out was as simple as it could be, consisting of a number of small circular and oval huts of timber.[15] Within half a century these had been burnt down and replaced by a new series of larger timber structures, the plan of which, although it clearly contained some rectangular elements, could not fully be determined. The familiar rectangular range of rooms in stone, later provided with wings and a linking portico, was built shortly after 180, and it survived in use down to the late third century. As was often the case, the main dwelling was sited within and to one side of a rectangular ditched enclosure, the ground immediately in front of the house perhaps representing the farm-yard. In the late third century, as a result of modestly increasing prosperity, a large aisled hall was added in one corner of the enclosure, overlying in part the boundary ditch. This new structure was certainly used as a dwelling at some time, since it had a group of small chambers at either end, those at the east end including a room heated by a hypocaust. It seems from the published plan,[16] however, as though at least two periods of occupation are represented here, and thus the earliest version of the structure may have had functions other than residential. Probably at about the same time, another building, known only from surface finds of building materials, was erected on the other side of the yard. Buildings which may have lain on the estate of the third-century villa are difficult to identify. An aisled building at Stubbins Wood,[17] 5 km. away to the north, may have been one of the subsidiary farms on the periphery of the villa land, but this must remain a hypothesis.

A recent study of all the pottery[18] from this villa reveals that there is very little material which must date from the fourth century. Not a single vessel can be certainly identified as belonging to the second half of the fourth century, and only a small number of sherds betoken occupation between 300 and 350. The only secure evidence for occupation of any kind after about 300 is a coin of Constantine I, found beneath stone paving at the east end of the aisled building. While occupation continued after A.D. 300, the villa seems to have been in greatly reduced circumstances.

Winterton[19] (fig. 18)

The lay-out of this well known north Lincolnshire villa is fairly similar to that of Mansfield Woodhouse in the spatial relationship of its subsidiary dwellings to the main dwelling. The principal interest of the recent excavations at Winterton, however, resides in the information they have provided on the buildings associated with the earlier occupation phases. These structures include a circular stone-founded hut, floored

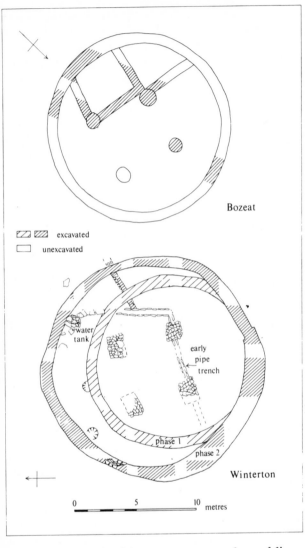

excavated
unexcavated

Bozeat

water
tank

early
pipe
trench

phase 1
phase 2

Winterton

0   5   10 metres

19. Plans of
stone
round-
houses:
Bozeat
(North-
ants)
and
Winterton
(Lincs.)

with mortar and with a quarter-round moulding covering the junction between wall and floor. The roof was supported by uprights resting on four post-bases of pitched stone, arranged in the form of a square and centrally placed within the hut. A very similar hut plan has been recorded at Bozeat (Northants.)[20] in the Nene valley (fig. 19). Two further stone buildings appear to have been circular or polygonal in plan. The structure with the four post-bases has been firmly dated to the second century, probably making way for an aisled building towards the end of that century. At this time the site was drastically re-planned. A simple rectangular block which had been a contemporary of the round hut was now adapted into the nave of an aisled building, aisles being added to its exterior, and the whole building being extended at one end. This aisled structure was certainly designed, in part at least, as a dwelling, a small room at one end having plastered walls and floor. The function of the original rectangular block is doubtful. In the opinion of its excavator it may have served as a byre. The ancillary buildings of no other Coritanian villa have been as carefully studied as these, and it would plainly be unwise at this stage to speculate whether they were typical or not. The occurrence of a fairly sophisticated form of round hut at a date which is certainly after A.D. 100 is a striking instance of the survival of older traditions of house-construction until long after the conquest. Other fairly late round huts in this part of Britain, at Bozeat (fig. 19) Thistleton Dyer and beneath the Great Weldon villa are reminders that virtually nothing has yet been learnt about what may be called the vernacular architecture of Roman Britain.

CLASS III

The humblest class, the aisled dwellings and the smaller portico-houses, will probably turn out to be the largest class of all. Two instances which have been recently excavated are those at Denton (fig. 20) and Empingham.[21] The earliest phase of the Denton house took the form of a timber hall, with a nave separated from flanking aisles by a double row of timber uprights. Its date is noticeably late: constructed about 300, it remained in use until about 370. About that date the western part of the hall was rebuilt, stone foundations and tessellated floors now being laid. This end of the building now and probably earlier served as domestic quarters, the remainder being most likely devoted to the storage of farm equipment and fodder. A hundred metres away from the

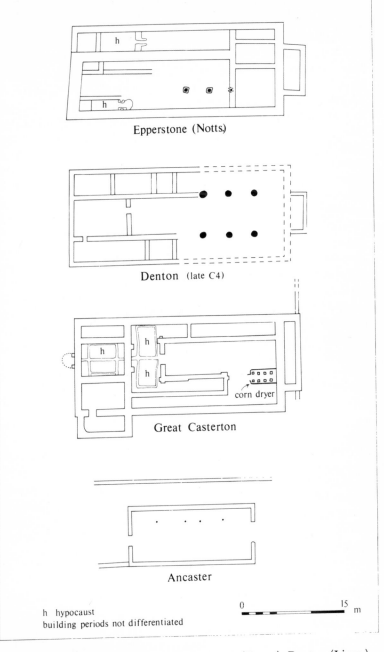

Epperstone (Notts.)

Denton (late C4)

Great Casterton

corn dryer

Ancaster

h hypocaust
building periods not differentiated

0   15
          m

20. Plans of aisled farmhouses at Epperstone (Notts.), Denton (Lincs.),
Great Casterton (Rutland), and Ancaster (Lincs.)

house, a small bath-house was now,[22] or a little later, erected, and in due course the stone foundations and tessellated floors of the dwelling were extended to take in the east end of the north aisle, leaving the south side still in timber.

Empingham, in the little valley of the Gwash, provides an interesting example of two contemporary aisled buildings, 300 metres apart and separated by the river. At least one other building lay nearby. No late Iron Age or early Roman occupation is attested. This complex seems to represent internal colonization of the valley from the second half of the second century onward. There is no trace of a neighbouring 'great house'.

Taken as a whole, the aisled dwellings independent of another house are particularly common in the southern parts of the tribal area, in south Lincolnshire, the Welland valley, Rutland and Northamptonshire. Although their detailed distribution over the whole province has not yet been worked out,[23] this is one area where one can speak of a concentration of them. As is well known, they appear to have no antecedents in Iron Age Britain or in the adjacent Roman provinces of Gaul and Germany. Nor is there good reason to derive them from the familiar timber aisled halls of free Germany. They are best viewed as an insular development of the Roman period.

The standards of life demonstrated by them are scarcely higher than those of many peasant or 'native' settlements. Probably that is what many of these aisled villas really are,[24] although others may well represent subsidiary units within large estates. Here we are at the mercy of our entirely archaeological evidence, which can say nothing about the crucial matter of land-ownership. Both Empingham and Denton, for example, could be either independent farms or parts of larger *fundi*.

Chronology of villas

Although the subject needs much more work, a few remarks may be ventured on the available evidence for the chronology of villas. Of the ten villas which have been carefully examined, most began their life at a relatively late date. There is no certain case of any villa foundation before about 125. As yet only Mansfield Woodhouse and Norton Disney[25] have produced evidence of fairly intensive occupation in the first century, and in both cases this was associated with timber huts and not with rectangular stone cottages like the first stone phases at Lockleys and Park Street.[26] It is not until the later second century that developed villa plans emerged, the clearest cases being the sites of Mansfield Woodhouse and Winterton. At the latter site, as has been outlined above, the earliest villa emerged after a prolonged occupation of stone huts built in a pre-Roman tradition, and the timber hut phase at Mansfield Woodhouse may likewise continue well into the second century. Several villas were not established before the late third or fourth centuries (Great Casterton,[27] Denton and Empingham in its developed form). These late foundations presumably indicate important developments in the internal colonisation of the region in the palmiest days of Romano-British agriculture.

The latest phase in the history of many Coritanian villas is the most difficult to evaluate, but it should be noted that a significant number have produced little or no evidence for occupation after about 350. This group includes Epperstone, Empingham, Barton in Fabis, Mansfield Woodhouse, Norton Disney, Southwell. Indeed, only the two late foundations of Denton and Great Casterton *certainly* continued down to at least the end of the fourth century. These preliminary remarks are based on very scanty evidence and must be open to reconsideration as information is produced by fresh excavations. The scarcity of later fourth century finds, however, does seem to be reliably attested in all these cases and should earn due attention. The phenomenon is difficult to account for, unless it is a result of a radical reorganization of land-ownership during the later fourth century, possibly caused by the amalgamation of estates. This would be in line with what was happening elsewhere in the western provinces at this time, but there is no certainty that it was happening in Britain.

Chronology of the Best-recorded Villa-sites

	A.D. 50	100	150	200	250	300	350	400
Barton in Fabis			————————————					
Denton							————	
Empingham				—————————				
Epperstone	. . . .			————————				
Great Casterton							————	
Great Weldon	. . . .		————————————————					
Mansfield Woodhouse	. . . . .		————————————————					
Norton Disney	. . . . .		————————————————					
Southwell	. . .		————————————————					
Winterton	. . . .		————————————————					

. . . . Earlier occupation, usually in timber huts or stone round-houses.

————————————— Villa occupied

Note

This table reproduces the results of an examination of the pottery from all of these ten sites with the exception of Winterton. No doubt further excavation will greatly improve the accuracy of the record. At present it can serve only as a rough guide. The starting dates of some sites, e.g. Barton in Fabis, Epperstone, and Southwell may well prove to be earlier than I have shown them here.

There are many outstanding gaps which more excavation can be expected to fill. One of these concerns villa-outbuildings and associated fields and enclosures. Only two sites have produced good evidence for paddocks and enclosures in their environs, and they are Cromwell (Notts.) and Winterton (Lincs.).[28] At Cromwell, air photographs reveal a small portico-villa standing at the centre of a rectangular, double-ditched enclosure (fig. 21). Within this, there are many small closes, some of which may have been stock-pounds, others orchards and gardens. Outside the main enclosure, there are other ditched plots, but no absolutely clear trace of a contemporary field-system. Air photographs of the environs

21. The Roman villa at Cromwell (Notts.) and its closes

of the Winterton villa show a planned system of regularly sized rectangular plots, of a size appropriate to stock-pounds rather than fields (fig. 22).

Information about outbuildings is still sparse. Several villas, including Mansfield Woodhouse, Norton Disney and Winterton, had ancillary aisled buildings which served as dwellings-cum-barns, but not evidently as dwellings-cum-byres. Great Weldon[29] had about its central yard a series of sheds without subdivisions which could have housed small numbers of stock as well as fodder and equipment, but elsewhere byres and animal pens are conspicuous by their scarcity. This at first sight may seem perplexing. But it may be that most of the sheep and cattle spent all their time in the open, in summer on river-pastures and in winter in closes near to the villa. On the drier, eastern side of Britain such a proceeding is possible, particularly if the cattle are being reared for meat rather than for milk. At a few sites, certain features of the outbuildings are baffling. At Great Casterton, for instance,[30] a free-standing wall ran off from the corner of an aisled building for an unknown distance and destination (fig. 23). From one end of the other house, a pair of walls defining a corridor about 3 metres wide ran on for about 24 metres, and the more northerly of the two for at least 60 metres. The impression given by the plan is of a large courtyard to the north-east of the excavated buildings, which may thus have formed only part of a much larger complex.

To some degree associated with this gap is the near-total absence of information about the economy of the villas. On this, Coritanian villas have as yet virtually nothing to contribute. One approach to the problem of finding out more may be framed as a question. Was the basic economy of the villa necessarily any different from that of peasant agriculture? It is generally held that villas represent a particular kind of farming: 'in the Roman villa we are considering a specific and peculiar method of exploiting the land.'[31] This view has been virtually unchallenged since Collingwood first postulated 'two economic systems existing side by side', one based on villas, the other on 'native' settlements. What evidence is there for this, and if there is none, is it a necessary postulate? For the region with which we are dealing there is

22. Enclosures in the vicinity of the villa at Winterton (Lincs.)

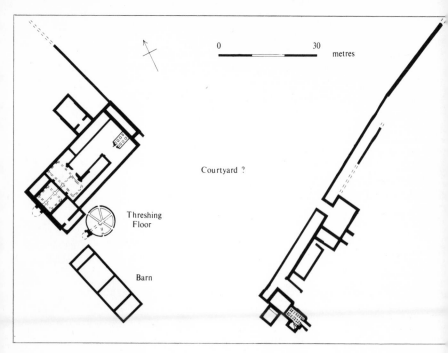

Threshing
Floor

Courtyard ?

Barn

23. Plan of the villa at Great Casterton, Rutland

simply no evidence for the kind of farming which sustained the villas and we can therefore only speculate whether it was necessarily different *in essentials* from that practised by the peasants. If the large villas are taken as a starting-point, they at least must have depended upon something much more profitable than mixed farming not far above subsistence level. Stock-rearing is the likeliest source of such wealth, since so little profit could come from arable farming. The moderately prosperous villas, like Winterton, Great Weldon and Mansfield Woodhouse, must also have been supported by something more than arable agriculture. But what of the farms here distinguished as Class III ? If numbers of these were indeed independent units, as is here assumed, need their modest architectural pretensions indicate anything other than the increasing wealth of an active peasant family? Even a narrow profit margin would be enough to allow the construction of a rectangular aisled hall to replace circular timber huts. In sum, it may be false to seek a homogeneous 'villa economy' behind *all* villas. The humbler seats may have been much closer to peasant settlements in the matter of economy than to the great houses. Whatever the truth, a vast amount of work is needed before the 'villa economy' emerges as something more than a learned construction.

Peasant settlements

The humbler farming settlements — 'native' or peasant settlements as they are commonly termed — present an even sorrier picture than the villas. Air photography has revealed an enormous number (figs. 24 & 27) especially in the valleys of the Trent and Welland (fig. 25) but very few have been excavated: not one has been totally examined. The difficulties attending study of these sites prove a powerful deterrent to most excavators. Their slight remains are not informative unless excavated on a large scale — and even their plan may be patchy and incoherent. Often dating is difficult because nondescript local wares predominate. Once again the greatest gap is the absence of information about their economy.

Sites of this kind carry Iron Age characteristics deep into the Roman period — perhaps in some cases throughout it — and therefore we can fitly start with settlements which date from shortly before and shortly after the Conquest. A considerable number of late Iron Age farms are known on the Welland gravels east of Stamford, several of them continuing under occupation into the Roman period. The most fully studied are the sites at Tallington (Lincs.).[32] Here a single Iron Age hut, 4.6 metres in internal diameter and set in a rectangular enclosure of 1.4 hectares, was later succeeded by another farmstead represented by a much smaller enclosure. This contained two working hollows, where such tasks as cooking, threshing and milling might have been performed, a timber granary and racks to contain hay or straw. The living quarters also presumably lay within the enclosure, probably in an area destroyed by gravel quarrying. This complex of remains seems to give us a typical single farm of the period *c*. 40-90. A pollen sample from a nearby site, of similar date and character, contains evidence to suggest that there had been considerable clearance of the tree

24. Complex of enclosures and other crop-marks on the Trent gravels, north of South Muskham (Notts.)

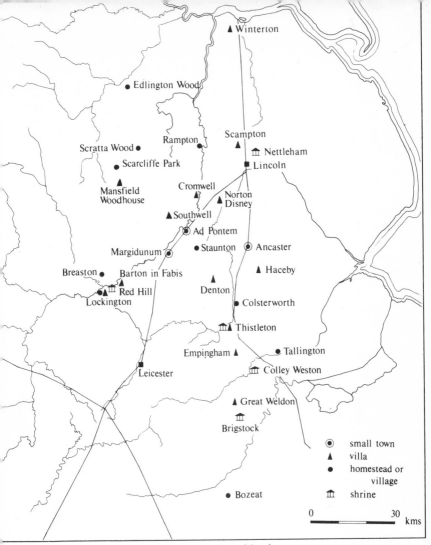

25. Rural sites mentioned in the text

cover in this area by the later first century. Grass pollens made up 47% of the total, those of trees and shrubs only 7%.[33] Probably a mixed farming economy was practised, on a basis of stock-rearing and grain growing. In essentials, this may not have been so different from the economy of many of the smaller villas already discussed.

Farms of this type were thickly concentrated on the river terraces all over the Lowland Zone. On the Trent gravels enormous numbers of such sites are known, almost entirely from air photography. We are still desperately short of well excavated sites, but the air photographs[34] suggest the existence of both single homesteads and small clusters of circular huts within rectilinear enclosures. Usually other enclosures without traces of huts occur in association, these presumably being paddocks and small fields. Such excavation as has taken place indicates a broad continuity in material life between the Iron Age and the Roman occupation. Roman objects circulated in this *milieu* freely, but in other respects life was unaltered. Of such farmsteads, the only excavated instances in the Trent valley to date are examples at Breaston, Willington (Derbys.), and Rampton (Notts.).[35] At Rampton a rather small hut, some 5.2 m. in diameter, stood on the alluvium on a site which would leave it vulnerable to winter floods. Its date is about the time of the Roman conquest, but a complicated series of boundary ditches nearby make it clear that occupation continued here down to the fourth century. A farmstead of a slightly later date has been recorded at Breaston (fig. 26). This settlement consists of a number of huts, three at least, lying within a ditched enclosure of about 1.6 ha. This is probably the holding of a single family group or a number of small family units, resembling the site at Colsterworth (fig. 4), which Professor Grimes dates to about the time of the Conquest (above, p. 6). Like the Welland valley sites already mentioned, the Trent farmsteads seem to have depended upon a mixed farming economy.

There is growing appreciation that nucleated peasant settlements existed in Lowland Britain as well as in the Highland Zone. The most striking instance among the Coritani of a sizeable peasant village is the settlement at Lockington (Leics.).[36] Though still unexcavated, it raises several interesting possibilities (fig. 27). The site lies on the Trent flood-plain close to the confluence with the Soar. On either side of a long droveway there lie some twenty circular huts, most of them within or adjacent to ditched enclosures of varying size. The overlapping of features indicates that not all these enclosures and dwellings are contemporary, but the unifying droveway makes it certain that we are dealing with a small community of families and not with a succession of single steadings. Less than 200 metres away to the east there

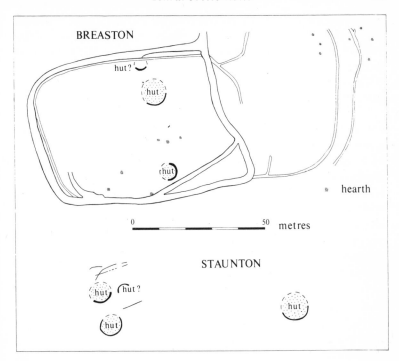

26. Plans of peasant settlements at Breaston (Derbyshire) and Staunton (Notts.)

lies a small villa, and the relationship of that establishment to the village invites speculation. There has been no excavation here as yet, but surface finds from the site of the village suggest that some of the huts at least were occupied as late as the second century and probably later. If this is so, it may well be that these are the homes of tenants or serfs farming the villa-estate. The other possibility is that the village preceded the villa, and that a change in land tenure took place during the Roman period. Whatever the reality, it is rare to have the opportunity to pose questions of this kind, and excavation at Lockington is consequently more than usually desirable.

On the heavier lands of the Boulder Clay and Keuper Marl not a single peasant homestead has yet been examined on an adequate scale. The only site which comes near to providing a satisfying record is that at Staunton in the Vale, near the northern edge of the Vale of Belvoir (fig. 26).[37] The Staunton farmstead consisted of a small group of roughly circular timber huts, not evidently associated with enclosures. All these simple dwellings, not more than four in number, had been occupied in the late-third or fourth century. Occupation on the site, or nearby, had begun certainly by about 100 and a few sherds of what may be Iron Age pottery were also recovered, but no buildings associated with this early period were found. Even as late as the fourth century the quality of life evinced by the surviving remains was at the humblest level. Small objects apart from pottery were very sparse. Even such commonplace things as iron nails, bronze studs and brooches were rarities. The picture is of a small unit of people living at the lowest social level. In the fourth century, such conditions were appropriate to the settlements of *coloni* or slaves attached to a large estate.

In the Pennine foothills, settlements of a distinctive upland type occur. These are close in physical character to those of the Yorkshire Pennines and the Northumberland hills, but whether their economy was essentially different from that of sites in the river valleys is still not clear. The three best known sites are those at Edlington Wood near Doncaster, Scarcliffe Park near Langwith (Derbys.) and Scratta Wood near Worksop (Notts.).[38] That at Scratta Wood consists of at least one oval enclosure, about 30 m. by 23, bounded by a dry-stone wall. Within it lay the huts of a small community living only slightly above the lowest distinguishable level, using relatively little pottery and possessing few objects of iron and bronze. The site had been occupied before the Conquest, but the detailed history of the Iron Age settlement cannot be outlined.

A group of more than six enclosures at Edlington Wood, 5 km. south-west of Doncaster, is to date the largest recorded group of these settlements. Near the enclosures stand rather small rectangular buildings in stone, the largest of which measure no more than 12.6 by 6.6 m. These were occupied in the second and third centuries, there being, surprisingly, no trace of fourth-century occupation material. Whether this group of dwellings was associated with a large estate or

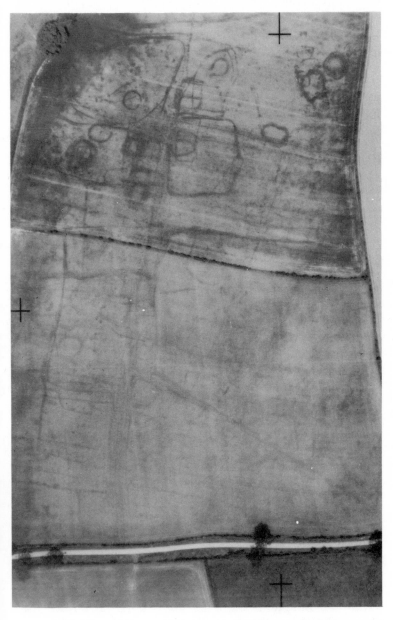

27. The peasant settlement at Lockington (Leics.)

represents a community of free peasants is unknown.

Two further manifestations of peasant settlement will help to fill out this outline sketch. Neither has been systematically studied, but both may have had considerable local significance. The one concerns a number of small hill-forts in south Nottinghamshire, within which peasant communities maintained themselves for a considerable length of time during the Roman period. There has been no excavation within the defences of any of these forts, but in at least one case, Fox Wood near Calverton, the Roman buildings included at least one rectangular structure in stone. The other form of settlement is the use by peasants of caves and rock-shelters in the limestone country of north-east Derbyshire.[39] This sounds like a desperate measure on the part of impoverished and unenterprising people. The finds from several caves, however, reveal that their inhabitants were far from impoverished and this recourse to natural shelters is better interpreted as indicating the readiness of countrymen to utilise every natural advantage to the full.

The rural shrines

A description of the countryside would not be complete without some account of the rustic shrines, since apart from their use as places of religious observance, these shrines often served as the sites of markets or fairs. Close to the southern border of the *civitas* there were two groups of Romano-Celtic temples, at Colley Weston and at Brigstock.[40] Three buildings at Colley Weston, a hexagon, an octagon and a circular structure, were probably all shrines, but other buildings existed here, including a small dwelling (for a custodian?). The date at which the site was in use seems to have been the second and third centuries. At Brigstock, there were at least three shrines, two circular and one polygonal in plan (fig. 28). Both places lie well away from Roman towns, but at the heart of a widespread group of agricultural settlements. No clue to the identity of the deity or deities worshipped at Colley Weston was obtained in the excavations, but four statuettes of a horse and rider from Brigstock offer a clue to the character of the presiding deity

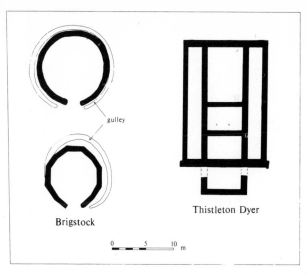

gulley

Brigstock

Thistleton Dyer

0   5   10 m

28. Plans of temples at Brigstock (Northants) and Thistleton Dyer (Rutland)

here. The rider has certain military attributes, a tall helmet and a cloak, which reveal him to be a warrior god, presumably surviving from a pre-Roman Celtic cult. Several other figurines of mounted warrior-gods have been found in the southern part of the canton, at Bourne, *Tripontium,* Westwood Bridge, and not far away at Willingham Fen (Cambs.).[41] Their occurrence in this area is too frequent to be coincidental.

Polygonal and round temples are by no means peculiar to the Coritani, or to Roman Britain. These Coritanian instances must be viewed, not as tribal peculiarities, but as manifestations of a common tradition of religious building shared by Celts on both sides of the Channel.

A much rarer kind of temple to be found in a rural context is that at the interesting site of Thistleton Dyer (fig. 28).[42] The earlier phases of the religious buildings in this extraordinary complex are represented by a timber circular structure of the first century A.D., succeeded by a stone building of similar plan. The presence of Iron Age pottery and 13 Coritanian coins suggests that the place may already

29. Inscription recording the dedication of an arch to the god Viridios: from Ancaster (Lincs.)

have had a religious significance before the Roman conquest. In the later third century, the circular temple was replaced by a large basilican temple of truly Classical plan, measuring 19.8 metres by 13.7 metres overall. Outside this remarkable building and set at right angles to it lay a large hall-like structure, which may have been a place of assembly connected with cult-festivals. A small silver plaque from a votive deposit within the basilican temple provides the only evidence for the deity worshipped here. The plaque is inscribed and records a dedication by one Mocuxsoma to the god Veteris. This is the first occurrence of this cult outside the military zone.

Another temple site, on the hill-top of Red Hill near Thrumpton (Notts.)[43] has been recently identified. From it came three inscribed lead tablets, one of them a curse. Further shrines of the rural population are indicated by finds of inscriptions, religious sculpture and cult-objects. The most interesting of the inscriptions are those from Ancaster and from Nettleham, 4 km. north of Lincoln, both of which mention *arcus* — presumably in this context arches leading into shrines or sacred enclosures (fig. 29).[44] At Ancaster, the god commemorated was the otherwise unrecorded Celtic deity Viridios: at Nettleham, the *arcus* was associated with a sanctuary of Mars Rigonemetus, here mentioned for the first time in Romano-British records. The more important pieces of sculpture and the cult-objects include a stone relief from Keisby (Lincs.)[45] of a god or worshipper standing by an altar, a small lead figurine of a fertility goddess found at Calverton (Notts.),[46] and part of a bronze crown from Deeping St. James (Lincs.),[47] probably worn by a priest during cult ceremonies.

5.

Industry and the economy

When dealing with the industrial activities of a part of the Roman Empire, it is vital to avoid anachronism and to banish all modern notions of how industry is conducted. The Roman Empire produced nothing approaching an industrial society. Much Roman industry, like the industries of medieval Europe, was carried on by individual craftsmen and by single families catering for a relatively small market. Goods ranging from agricultural machinery to ear-rings would normally be ordered to individual specifications and collected by the purchaser when ready. Large-scale industry in the modern sense is really encountered only in the fields of mining, quarrying and pottery-making — and at least in the last-named case there was a great deal of production by local craftsmen. In this chapter it is proposed to examine the major industries carried on in the region: iron-extraction and working, stone-quarrying, salt-production, and pottery-making. The abundant evidence for minor crafts requires much more space than is here available.

The iron industry

One of the major *pretia victoriae* for the Romans in the east Midlands was the mineral wealth of the region (fig. 30). Outstanding among those mineral deposits were the lead of Derbyshire and the iron-stone of the Jurassic ridge, and both will have been rapidly exploited by the invaders. The lead field of south and central Derbyshire lies outside Coritanian territory and, in any case, in the early years it lay under direct military supervision. The iron-stone will thus be our main concern in the sphere of metals.

The organization of the iron industry in Roman Britain as a whole is little known. The areas where iron-mining was carried on were probably not thought to demand that degree of administration and control accorded to the iron-mines of Gaul and Noricum, or to the lead and silver deposits of Britain herself. No *procuratores ferrariarum* are recorded in Britain, and official control may have been confined to military supervision of certain iron-fields which were conveniently situated for the purposes of military supply.[1] Elsewhere, the native miners and smiths seem to have arranged matters to their own liking.

Iron formed one of the main sources of the region's wealth long before the Roman conquest, and working of the deposits will have been well advanced before A.D. 43. As has already been observed, the iron-stone deposits may have been an important factor influencing the pattern of Iron Age settlement.[2] Certainly there are noticeable clusters of pre-Roman occupation sites in areas where the iron-stone outcrops, notably in south-west Lincolnshire, Rutland and the adjacent parts of Leicestershire, and the north-west corner of Lincolnshire.[3] Virtually every part of the northern reaches of the Jurassic ridge is rich in iron-stone and it is therefore not surprising to find abundant evidence for Romano-British exploitation of this staple material. Unfortunately, the evidence has usually come to light during fast-moving modern mining of the same deposits and there has rarely been scope for careful observation. As a result, the information provided by the known smelting-sites is of very uneven quality. The principles and the technical processes of smelting have been fully discussed by R.F. Tylecote and the reader is referred to his detailed account.[4] Both the main types of smelting-furnace so far known from Roman Britain, the simple bowl-hearth and the more sophisticated shaft-furnace, have been recorded in the region. A bowl hearth, dated to the Flavian period, was found within the walls of Great Casterton[5] and several others have been briefly recorded during open-cast mining at Thealby and Bagmoor in north Lincolnshire.[6] These hearths are no more than shallow

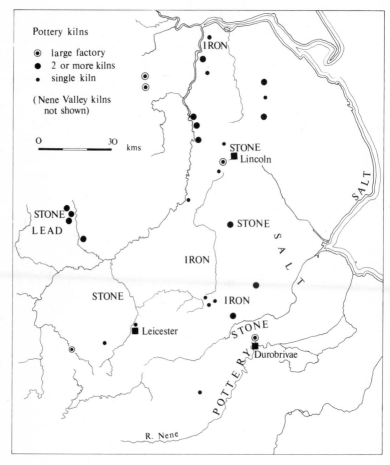

30. Sites of industrial working

hollows into which, after they have been packed with ore, a draught of air was introduced, probably by means of bellows. The blooms of iron which resulted had to be reheated and hammered, so that the considerable slag-residue could be removed.

The more advanced shaft-furnace, of which the best known Romano-British examples are those from Ashwicken (Norfolk),[7] is a relatively recent addition to our knowledge of Roman iron technology. A group of three such furnaces at

Pickworth (Rutland),[8] three km. east of Ermine Street, provides the only known instances among the Coritani. These three furnaces, two of which were excavated, stood in a straight line with a 2.5 metres interval between them. Probably their original height was at least 1.5 metres. In a furnace of this height, the necessary flow of air would follow naturally and a much larger mass of ore could be smelted at one time than in a bowl hearth. Pottery and traces of a simple shelter were found nearby, but this interesting installation is close to no known villa or settlement of any kind.

Rather more problematic is the furnace from Colsterworth (Lincs.),[9] found in 1931 and well known as one of the first Romano-British smelting furnaces to be carefully examined. This structure, which lay in a hollow 2.13 m. across and 1.22 m. deep, consisted of a rectangular box of fired clay, 61 cm. by 76 cm. and 58 cm. high, with large openings to front and rear, and a hole 15 cm. in diameter in each side. Smaller holes, made with the finger and closed by sherds of pottery, occurred in the roof. Associated with this odd furnace were a number of burnt clay bars, resembling the fire-bars of a pottery kiln, 7 by 6 cm. in section and 46 cm. long. Although long accepted as a smelting furnace, the method by which iron might have been produced in this unusual contraption remains obscure. The burnt clay bars, in particular, are inexplicable in the context of iron-smelting. Dr Tylecote's opinion is that it did not produce iron, but that it possibly could have been used to make steel by carburising iron already smelted. This puzzling installation remains unique.

Within a short distance of Pickworth and Colsterworth there lies a third iron-smelting site, at Clipsham (Rutland),[10] where large mounds of iron slag and ash, associated with stone buildings, were exposed in the 1920s and again shortly before 1940. Unfortunately, no satisfactory records of this important find appear to have been made and no further excavation has been undertaken on their site. Possibly the Roman settlement at nearby Market Overton was also concerned with iron-working, but this poorly recorded site is yet another which calls for modern excavation.

In the Nene valley, the environs of *Durobrivae* have much

to reveal of the iron industry. At a little distance to the north of the walled town, at Bedford Purlieus,[11] furnaces for the roasting of ore have been identified and further up the valley at Oundle and near Irchester there were other workings of some importance. The deposits in the hills overlooking the Vale of Belvoir were also exploited, and no doubt many more smelting sites will eventually be added to the sole instance yet recorded here, that at Goadby Marwood (Leics.).[12]

Enough is known, then, of the distribution of sites where smelting was carried on to indicate the main areas of iron-mining.[13] How the industry was organized and administered is obscure, and in the absence of direct literary or epigraphic evidence it is asking too much of the archaeological evidence to supply the answer. The relationship of the furnaces to settlements is still either impossible or difficult to establish, but the scanty evidence is still worth reviewing. The large slag dumps at Clipsham lie close to buildings, but it is not clear what these were, or whether they were solely concerned with the working of iron. They may represent a humble farm. The Pickworth and Colsterworth furnaces lie close to no known settlement, and thus while they may indicate an industrial concern of some competence and ambition, the headquarters of such a concern are elusive, unless the villa and settlement at Thistleton Dyer[14] played that role. The ill-recorded smelting sites of Thealby, Bagmoor and Scawby in north-west Lincolnshire may well have been associated with villa estates rather than with an industrial complex, but this cannot be proved.[15] Only one villa, that at Great Weldon (Northants.), has so far yielded evidence of iron-working on a large scale. Excavation here has produced several large lumps of cinder, the largest of which weighed about 80 lbs.[16] But even this smelting may have been connected only with the working of a large agricultural estate. Many other sites where smelting has been attested, for instance at Goadby Marwood, Claxby (Lincs.) and Bringhurst (Northants.),[17] may represent no more than the production of iron for local agricultural use, perhaps on a single estate.

The stone quarries

The winning of stone for building must have played a much more important role in the industrial affairs of the region that the surviving evidence at first suggests. As in the case of other mineral deposits, much has been destroyed by post-Roman working of the same deposits, so much in fact that it is not possible to affirm the Roman origin of any quarry or group of quarries, even though in several cases there is a strong presumption in their favour. In these circumstances, the only evidence at our command comes from study of the stone used in excavated buildings and of the products of associated crafts such as those of the architectural mason and the sculptor.[18] Even this evidence could be much more plentiful than it is. Excavators still frequently fail to record the building-stones represented on their sites and geologists have been all too rarely consulted as to whether the sources of the stone can be precisely located. While the material evidence is not extensive, however, there is enough to increase hopes for fresh finds and for more scrupulous recording of the old.

In most parts of lowland Britain, the greatly increased pace of building in stone from the second century onward called into being a flourishing industry in the quarrying and working of stone. Coritanian territory abounds in building-stone of high quality, the best of which has achieved a high fame through its use in medieval churches: Barnack rag, and the limestones of Ancaster and Ketton. The limestone of the Jurassic ridge assumes the most prominent position, of course, but there were other souces of good stone. The Carboniferous limestone of Derbyshire and the Millstone Grit of the same county enjoyed a more than local employment, the latter being in addition used in querns.[19] The granites and 'Slate' of Charnwood Forest[20] were also used outside their area of origin, the latter proving useful as a roofing material. But it is with the Jurassic limestones that a start must be made.

A major group of quarries lay to the north of *Durobrivae*. This group included the quarries of Barnack rag-stone, used not only in this region for buildings and for sculpture, but as far away as London.[21] In the medieval period, Barnack rag was transported in some quantity to East Anglia, its distribution-area being to a considerable degree influenced by the course of navigable rivers. There are hints that transport of Barnack stone in the Roman period had been in the same direction. For instance, a coffin in this material has been found at Icklingham (Suffolk) and another at Arbury Road, Cambridge,[22] and instances of its use in buildings are recorded at Godmanchester and Lords Bridge, near Cambridge.[23] Nearer to *Durobrivae* there were quarries (e.g. at Sibson and Alwalton) which yielded stone for purely local purposes.

Like those at Barnack, the Ketton quarries sent stone outside the region. It has been found at Verulamium,[24] and on the Cambridgeshire sites of Comberton, Ickleton and Swaffham Prior.[25] The excellent limestone in the vicinity of Ancaster was also worked, possibly on a scale not yet fully appreciated. Transport of the stone away from Ancaster has not yet been proved,[26] but the evidence of local workshops making stone coffins and producing carved pieces of some quality suggests that here lay the centre of an industry serving more than the small town of Ancaster itself. Relatively little information about the building-stones used at Lincoln has yet been gathered together, but it is very likely that the buildings of *Lindum* were composed of oolitic limestone quarried at no great distance from the city, some of it possibly at Greetwell. A smaller centre of limestone-quarrying was the settlement at Clipsham. This probably served only a local market: so far its stone has been recorded at nearby Thistleton Dyer and Market Overton.

The speed with which the Romans began to exploit the stone of the Jurassic ridge is astounding. A few early tombstones found in southern England, including two of soldiers who died at Colchester before A.D. 60, and that of the procurator Classicianus at London, who died after that date, are of oolite from either the Cotswolds or Northamptonshire.[27] The relatively easy lines of transport by water make the latter source the more likely.

As we noted earlier, the quarries on the Jurassic ridge are by no means the whole story. The ancient volcanic rocks of

Charnwood Forest were also exploited to a degree which is still underestimated. Granite, or syenite, from Enderby, Groby, Mount Sorrell and Markfield is fairly commonly encountered in buildings in Leicester,[28] including the public baths and the forum, and was also used in the city wall. 'Slate' from the Swithland quarries, also in Charnwood Forest, was also employed in the city wall, but the major use to which this stone was put appears to have been as a roofing material. Its distribution area has not yet been fully worked out, but since it includes Leicester, *Margidunum*, Thorpe, Ancaster, the Norton Disney (Lincs.) villa, and villas north of the Trent at Epperstone and Thurgarton, and probably at Great Staughton (Hunts.) it was evidently of considerable regional importance. Another 'slate' much used for roofs in the south of the region is the fissile, sandy limestone found at Colley Weston (Northants.). When first quarried this is often a bluish colour, but weathering processes turn it to its familiar attractive buff. Many sites in the valleys of Welland and Nene, and in Rutland and south Lincolnshire reveal its use in quantity. It is also recorded at Verulamium.

About other building materials little can yet be noted. Millstone Grit from unidentified Derbyshire quarries was used for architectural details in the baths, forum and other buildings at Leicester,[29] and this durable stone may have been far more widely used than appears at present. This is one of the raw materials used in another neglected industry of Roman Britain, the manufacture of querns. Of the other local building-stones, two or three out of several deserve special mention. Sites in the middle Trent valley commonly had buildings constructed in a fine-grained local sandstone, 'skerry' as it is generally called, which occurs in bands in the Keuper Marl and is frequently found on the surface. This stone, although durable, does not often occur in large pieces and thus cannot be easily worked: these properties permitted its use mainly in the lower courses of buildings. Almost all the stone used in the excavated buildings at Thorpe and *Margidunum*[30] was skerry. The rather soft sandstone found at the southern end of the Wolds in Lincolnshire, usually termed Spilsby Sandstone, was used in the Roman defences of Horncastle and probably served other settlements in south-east Lincolnshire. A possible quarry site is that at Holbeck, 5½ km. north-east of Horncastle. Elsewhere on the Wolds, Tealby Limestone and Chalk were at the disposal of local builders. All these stones, however, although easy to work, are not of the best quality, tending to weather quickly, and none of them is likely to have been employed outside their immediate area of origin.

An important branch of the industry, too little studied as yet, is that which concerned itself with sculpture and architectural carving. Some of the sculpture which issued from Coritanian workshops ranks with the best found anywhere in Roman Britain. The location of these workshops can only be guessed at, but this was primarily an urban craft and Lincoln and Leicester probably enjoyed primacy in this field. Lincoln has one of the finest of all Romano-British sculptures, a finely drawn figure of a youthful charioteer in bas relief (fig. 31). This has been seen as part of a relief commemorating games performed by a college of the aristocratic youths of the colony,[31] but more probably it comes from a tomb-monument. There can be no doubt, however, about its place of manufacture. It is made from the local limestone and must be the product of a sculptor working in Lincoln. The fine portrait bust in Ketton stone of a youth, found at Barwell (Leics.)[32] probably originated in a Leicester workshop (fig. 32). Its features are strongly reminiscent of certain portraits of Julio-Claudian princes: Professor Toynbee has gone so far as to suggest that it represents Britannicus.[33] Whether this is correct or not, it is clear that this piece is one of the earliest of surviving Romano-British sculptures, and it would be interesting to know the circumstances in which it was commissioned and made.

Less well known than the Lincoln and Leicester pieces is a group of remarkable statues from the borderlands of the Coritani and Catuvellauni. This includes two small figures of charioteers brandishing whips, from Bedford Purlieus,[34] and life-size statues of Hercules, Apollo and Minerva, from Sibson,[35] all of these in Barnack rag. There are several other pieces of quality from elsewhere in the limestone belt. An interesting local group comes from Ancaster and its sur-

31. The young charioteer from a tomb monument in Lincoln

rounding region, comprising mainly religious items. The most notable are the famous relief of the *Matres*,[36] a life-size draped statue of a male god or hero,[37] and a rather small female head, with a coiffure in an early third century style.[38] Many other individual items, such as the male portrait bust from Clarborough (Notts.),[39] now sadly lost, display a high competence in carving and cast an occasional ray of light on the classicizing tastes of the wealthier Coritani.

Salt manufacture

Several sectors of the east coast of England were, in the Iron Age and Roman periods, centres of production of salt by the evaporation of brine. One of these centres was the area of silt fen about the shores of the Wash, particularly the land to the south-east of Spalding, the coastal marshland of east Lincolnshire, and the western margins of the Fens.[40] A considerable number of production sites, or salterns, have recently been recorded close to the Car Dyke in south Lincolnshire and near other artificial channels in the Fenland. The importance of salt in antiquity, and in the medieval period, is easily overlooked today. It was the most efficient preservative known in the ancient world, particularly for meat and fish, and played an important part in certain industrial processes, including the preparation of leather. It has long been known that salt-production about the Wash began in the Iron Age. Professor Swinnerton's studies of the geology of the Lincolnshire coast[41] incidentally brought to light Iron Age pottery associated with salterns, some of which lay buried beneath seven feet of clay. Salterns are readily identified by the broken remains of clay vessels used to evaporate the brine, the crude clay supports for them, and the baked clay linings of the hollows in which the boiling-hearths had been set. The enormous number of salterns in south-east Lincolnshire and elsewhere in the Fenland reveals the size of the industry in its hey-day, the first two centuries A.D., and it is thus all the more tantalizing that it is difficult to grasp how it was organized. Many of the salterns occur on or close to settlement-sites. In such cases it is a fair assumption that the peasant inhabitants added salt-making to their farming activities, and it is not impossible that some communities were mainly dependent upon the production of salt for their livelihood. Other salterns, however, appear to be quite unassociated with specific settlements and their significance is difficult to determine. If much of the Fenland was indeed an Imperial estate, the salt-making could be explained as the exploitation by the *conductores saltus* of all the natural resources of the domain, for industry as well as agriculture could be the concern of a *saltus*. It must be further recalled that, as in the mines, both male and female convicts could be condemned to terms of hard labour in the salt-works:

32. The bust of a youth (Britannicus?) from Barwell (Leics.)

It is usual to condemn women, whether for life or for a term, to wait upon the convicts in the mines and similarly in the salt-works.[42]

Some of the Lincolnshire salterns, especially those well away from known settlements, may thus be relics of a grim industry, carried on by the lowest members of Roman society.

The evidence of date so far recovered suggests that the first and second centuries saw the most intensive manufacture of salt. The area where salterns are thickest on the ground has produced hardly any evidence of working after the early fourth century, and it must be concluded that by about 300 this industry was virtually moribund.

Coal mining

Although coal was certainly worked by the Romans in Britain,[43] it is relatively rarely recorded on sites in this region, and it is clear that it was never a common fuel in this part of the civil province. It does occur, however, on a number of settlements in and near the Fenland: this anomalous situation has already been commented on by Dr Webster.[44] The nearest coal-deposits to the Fens are those of south Nottinghamshire, the outcrops in the Erewash valley being the most accessible source to ancient miners. Analysis of the microspores in some of the Fenland finds of coal suggests an origin in the Nottinghamshire coal-field or possibly further north in Yorkshire. This strange contrast between the Fenland and the rest of the region cannot yet be explained. Conceivably the special conditions of Imperial ownership which obtained here, together with the excellent facilities for transport by water offered by the canal system in Lincolnshire, may ultimately be shown to be connected with the phenomenon, but at present the problem cannot be satisfactorily resolved. It is not easy to account for the rarity of coal elsewhere, unless at a time when timber was abundant, coal was an unpopular as well as an expensive fuel, as it was in the early Middle Ages.

Pottery manufacture

Inevitably, the industry which has revealed most in the way of its products and its manufacturing centres is that of pottery-making, and it is highly desirable that an account of the Coritanian manufactories be included here. One outstanding reason why it should be is the fact that it is now obvious that study of the Romano-British pottery industry can most profitably proceed along regional lines. The factor of regionalism and its influence upon the dating and distribution of pottery is no new concept, but only recently has the principle become so well established as to enter the canon governing current practice on the subject. Despite some seventy years of research, much more work is needed in this field, and concentration on regional wares should pay the highest dividends. It must be admitted at the outset that study of the east Midland potteries has not yet advanced very far. Of some fifty excavated kiln-sites, about ten have been adequately published and of those ten only four can be regarded as major production centres. Systematic examination of the mass of pottery from excavated sites has at last begun to allow distinction between those wares and forms which were strictly local, and those which were more widely traded. But much remains to be learnt and all that is offered here is an interim statement in a continuing programme of work.

Before proceeding with a chronological account of how the industry developed, it will be helpful to indicate the main categories of manufactory which seem to have operated. First, there were a few centres of mass production, turning out vessels in vast quantities, for export to many parts of the province. Pride of place goes to the great colour-coated industry established in the Nene valley during the second century, one of the largest and longest-lived of the centralised pottery industries in the western provinces.[4 5] Another concern working on a massive scale was that which produced mortaria and other wares in the area about Hartshill and Mancetter (Warwicks.)[4 6] from the earlier second century to the fourth. After these huge factories come a large number of smaller concerns, serving a regional market only. Good examples of this class are the factories at Cantley and Rossington Bridge, south-east of Doncaster, and the fourth century kilns at Swanpool, near Lincoln. Finally, the humblest class of potteries comprises kilns serving limited areas, individual towns, lesser settlements or even single estates. As instances, one may cite certain wares found in Leicester, which have a strongly marked individuality due to its manufacture in local kilns. In north Lincolnshire, there are kilns, as yet not investigated, which appear to be associated with individual villas.[47] This third category of centre is the least well studied, for the very reason that the products of such kilns were not outstandingly profuse nor widely distributed. Nor are we well informed about how these minor concerns were organized. Those established near towns were probably set up by professional potters. Others, particularly those in the depths of the countryside, may represent no more than the occasional or seasonal manufacture of vessels for basic household needs.

These categories are not intended to be hard and fast. Many kiln-sites cannot yet be placed with certainty in either the second or third group. Other potteries began their operation as local workshops and later extended their market to embrace a wide area. Thus, the potteries making Derbyshire Ware[48] began to serve a local market in the earlier second century, won a regional market within half a century and by the early fourth century were exporting their products to the northern military garrisons. The distinctions between sizes of workshops suggested above are intended to serve as a reminder that the pottery industry, perhaps more than any other, was carried on at various levels of competence and with varying degrees of organization.

In the current state of knowledge, the earliest stage in the development of the industry can be best studied in the pottery from a few early Roman forts and peasant settlements. As is to be expected, we encounter a continuance of Iron Age potting techniques and vessel-forms, a circumstance which creates difficulties in distinguishing between the wares of the pre-Conquest period and those of the years immediately afterwards. These difficulties may actually be insoluble,

Hallward Library - Issue Receipt

Customer name: Cowderoy, Charlotte

Title: The Cortian / Malcolm Todd
ID: 6000274497

Due: 23/04/2010 23:59

Total items: 1
26/02/2010 15:24

All items must be returned before the due date
and time.
The Loan period may be shortened if the item is
requested.

since many Iron Age potters probably continued working after A.D. 43 in an unchanged tradition. This is a matter to be taken seriously when attempting to date pottery on sites which were occupied without interruption from before the Roman conquest.

The early Roman garrisons, for instance at Longthorpe, Ancaster and Great Casterton,[49] used a range of wares in which native vessels figured largely. As at the contemporary forts of Hod Hill and Waddon Hill in Dorset, the troops depended heavily upon the local potters for their supplies of common cooking vessels. The imported vessels included finer table wares, especially samian, mortaria and containers for liquids, such as flagons and amphorae. Few kilns belonging to this early phase have yet been found. The only certain examples are those at Hardingstone (Northants.)[50] in the upper Nene valley, which have been interpreted as a response to the requirements of military units active in the area shortly after the invasion. However that may be, their floruit must be set in the period of conquest. Nowhere in the region at this time is there any sign of centralised industries and these are not to be suspected. Nor are there signs that the army either made its own pottery or supervised the pro-duction of particular wares destined for its own use.[51]

Within a few years after A.D.43 Roman and Romanised native wares began to enter the region, especially from the south-east. Small quantities of pottery came from further afield — from Gallia Belgica and the Rhineland. The rather soft fabrics characteristic of the later Iron Age, often well levigated clays containing finely pounded shell-grit, gradually disappeared and were largely replaced by harder grey fabrics. But the intrusive forms by no means entirely replaced those of the Iron Age tradition, and in the period from *c.* 50-70 native and imported vessel-forms jostled one another in Coritanian markets. The kiln-sites at Weston Favell (Northants.)[52] and Blackmore Thick (Northants.)[53] belong to this period and their products show clearly the merging of two streams, the one local and the other derived ultimately from the Gallo-Belgic tradition.

In the period before A.D. 100, the range of fabrics and forms was astoundingly wide, and this great variety is to be attributed to the activity of a large number of small workshops. But not all the kiln-sites can have been operating on a small scale, for at this time it is possible to discern the beginnings of fairly prolific workshops. One example out of several in the region is that centre (or centres) which made a distinctive calcite-gritted fabric, recently termed Trent Valley ware[54] after its main area of distribution (fig. 33).

The most significant development in the half-century from *c*. 70-120 was in the mass production of grey fabrics. These by this time had replaced the softer calcite-gritted wares as the dominant element in common domestic pottery. It is difficult to pick out distinctive fabrics from this mass of wares, but it may be noted that the common decorative treatment known as rustication enjoyed its greatest vogue in this period. Kiln-sites producing it have been recorded at Dragonby, Lea, North Hykeham (all Lincs.)[55] and probably Leicester.[56] Local manufacture of colour-coated wares can now be detected,[57] but these made no prominent showing until the mid-second-century.

Although many details have still to be filled in, it is clear that between *c*. 120 and 150 there began great advances in the organization of certain potteries. Factories working on a massive scale opened in the Nene Valley about 150 and these rapidly developed into the most extensive and prosperous industrial complex in the whole province. Almost immediately, markets were won all over the Midlands, the South, and among the military garrisons of the North. Between 150 and 200, production of very similar colour-coated vessels began elsewhere in the east Midlands, e.g. at Great Casterton and South Carlton.[58] This process may have been stimulated by some potters migrating from the Nene valley. But the *diaspora* did not weaken the factories centred on *Durobrivae*. If anything, they continued to increase in size and prosperity.

Two other large factories began output on a massive scale in the early and middle decades of the second century. The one is the factory centred on Cantley and Rossington Bridge,[59] which produced mainly kitchen wares in grey fabrics, and mortaria. The latter were exported to north Britain, but there is remarkably little evidence for the grey wares away from the kilns: probably they did not travel

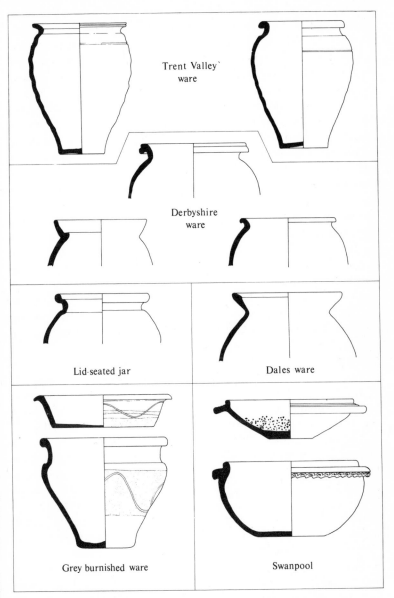

Trent Valley` ware

Derbyshire ware

Lid-seated jar

Dales ware

Grey burnished ware

Swanpool

33. Selected pottery products of East Midland workshops

outside the region. The other is the Hartshill-Mancetter factory in the south-west of the canton. This now began to turn out large quantities of mortaria,[60] which were exported all over the Midlands and the North and which reached the South in small numbers. At least one Hartshill potter, Sarrius, also worked at Rossington Bridge, having either migrated thither or having set up a branch workshop.

These huge enterprises are by no means the whole story. The workshops which made the heavy, overfired vessels known as Derbyshire Ware began operating about 120,[61] increased their scope later in the second century and by the early fourth century, if not earlier, they had won a small market among the northern garrisons. Two other east Midland jar types seem to have had similar success. The so-called Dales Ware form and a distinctive lid-seated jar appeared in the second half of the second century, the latter having a distribution area based on central Lincolnshire, the former being commoner in the north of that county and in south Yorkshire.[62] In the same period, the pottery found at both Leicester and Lincoln displays strong individual features, probably because it was produced by kilns serving each of the two cities and their surrounding territories.

The third century state of the industry is very imperfectly understood. Probably there were few major changes in the siting of production-centres. Since workshops established in the Antonine period seem still to have continued their activity, many vessel-forms which had emerged in the later second century remained in circulation until well on into the third, causing great difficulties for the archaeologist in the matter of chronology. After about 250, however, many new types began to appear and some of these were probably issued by new workshops not yet located. The commonest of these new wares are the high quality grey fabrics termed East Midland burnished wares.[63] These were to form a major component of the pottery of this region in the late third and early fourth centuries.[64]

The first half of the fourth century saw, by and large, a prolongation of the late third century industry. The large factories of the Nene valley and of Warwickshire were still working on a huge scale, and now the Lincoln potteries extended their market. The Swanpool-Boultham kilns,[65] in particular, greatly increased their output in the middle decades of the century, distributing their wares over the central part of the tribal territory.

How long the centralised factories and the smaller workshops lasted is difficult to assess. That of the Nene valley and probably the Lincoln group of kilns either escaped the devastation of 367-9 or quickly revived after the Theodosian restoration. The pottery of the very end of the fourth and the early fifth century, however, cannot be clearly distinguished from vessels of about 370, and while this stumblingblock remains, there is little hope for advance in this crucial subject. Possibly local wheel-made wares went on being made until about 420, but hardly later. About this time, Anglo-Saxon wares were beginning to spread over the region, and no doubt began to be used by British communities. In these conditions, the occasional hybrid[66] need cause no surprise. They signal the end of the Romano-British industry.

6.

The late fourth and fifth centuries

While there is much still to be learnt about the last years of Roman rule in the territory of the Coritani, archaeology is gradually making it clear that Roman forms of organization died slowly. Roman Britain did not suddenly collapse. Rather, it fell into pieces and some of those pieces defied total absorption or conquest by the Anglo-Saxons for a long time. As is to be expected, the Coritanian region shared in the general reorganization of the British provinces in the later fourth century,[1] though there is no evidence that military garrisons were established on permanent inland sites, as at early fourth-century Elslack and Newton Kyme in south Yorkshire.[2] The role that Horncastle and Caistor might have played in the new dispositions has already been discussed,[3] but it is, above all, in the towns that we can discern the latest structural changes in the Roman defence of the region. Many (if not most) walled towns in Roman Britain had their defences modified during the final period of Roman administration by the addition of projecting towers to their walls and, often as a necessary concomitant, by the provision of very wide ditches outside them. It has long been known that small projecting towers of roughly square plan at their footing were added to the angles of the polygonal circuit of Great Casterton (fig. 34).[4] More recently, it has been learnt that towers were also added to the angles of the Ancaster defences.[5] These had a peculiar fan-shaped plan, in which the front and back of the tower curved to match the curve of the wall to which they had been attached (fig. 34). Although the Ancaster towers are not closely dated, they may be presumed

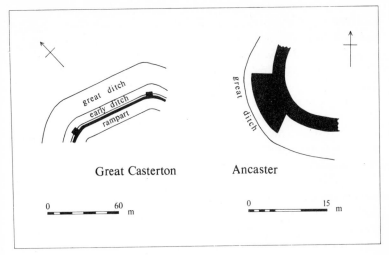

34. Towers in late fourth-century town defences

to have been a part of Theodosius' scheme of restoration. No other fortification in the region (apart from those of Horncastle and Caistor already mentioned) is yet known to have been provided with towers. No certain evidence for them has come from either Lincoln or Leicester,[6] although in neither case have the crucial points on the circuit been fully studied. Nor have towers been specifically sought at Thorpe, *Margidunum* or Brough, and it would be unwise to claim that in any of these three places their existence is precluded.

An interesting earthwork at Scaftworth, near Bawtry (Notts.),[7] sited near a crossing of the river Idle, may also belong to the Theodosian recovery. This little rectangular work, less than 0.4 ha. within the innermost of its three ditches, appears on a map of Nottinghamshire published in 1774, but thereafter disappeared from view until its redis-covery from the air in 1943. All three of its ditches have shallow profiles. The innermost has almost rectangular corners, while the outer pair are more gently rounded at the angles. Evidence for its dating is scanty, since excavation has so far been confined to sections across the defences. What there is points to the second half of the fourth century and probably to the period after 370. The position of the Scaftworth fortlet suggests that it was placed here to assist the policing of the important route[8] leading from the Trent valley towards *Danum* and thence into the Vale of York. Presumably other road-side fortlets of this kind remain to be found.

Apart from this very modest amount of information, there is little else to show how the towns and other settlements were faring at the end of the fourth century. Those equipped with defences will have had little to fear from barbarian raiders at this time: the open settlements had good reason to decline and many of them were probably abandoned in the late fourth and early fifth centuries. Nevertheless, here and there in the countryside there are (in the first half of the fifth century) striking glimpses of a still flourishing agricultural system of a recognizeable Romano-British kind. The villas at Denton, Great Weldon and Great Casterton[9] all survived until well into the century, the last-named producing the most telling structural evidence. This villa had been first established early in the fourth century on a site never previously occupied, some 900 metres from the defended village on Ermine Street. The earliest farm buildings, comprising an aisled hall, threshing-floor and cart-shed, were put up shortly after 300 and remained in use for at least half a century. After about 350, this group of buildings was demolished and replaced by a new series. The site of the aisled hall was employed for a small dwelling, originally of one room only, but later enlarged by the addition of two others. A further range of rooms linked by a corridor was now constructed, 46 metres away to the south. Many alterations and repairs were carried out on these two buildings after 370, including the insertion of heated rooms, and clearly the prosperity of this farm endured without major setback beyond the end of the fourth and, probably, well into the fifth century. When the end came, it was accompanied by an intense fire which destroyed several parts of the complex but even this did not terminate use of the site, for a small corn-drying floor was thereafter built into the ruined structure. The final destruction of the buildings did not therefore end all agricultural use of the place. Presumably those who were now tilling the land lived within the walled village.

Other rural sites have produced nothing to rival this remarkable case of the survival of Romano-British agricultural tradition in an area only 48 km. from the Wash, a likely landfall for both raiders and settlers. It remains true, however, that embarrassingly few villas and farmsteads have yet been studied with even elementary care. It is probably no coincidence that the three villas at which a late-fourth-century and early-fifth-century phase is evident, Denton, Great Weldon and Great Casterton, have all been treated to careful and recent excavation.

When deprived of sites, the archaeologist must turn to objects. Before leaving the Romano-British evidence it will be useful to survey what is known about the final phase of two major industries, pottery-making and metalwork.

The mass-producing pottery factories did not continue working for long after 400. Some suffered a major set-back in the disastrous years 367-9, others ended their activity at that time. But since there is widespread agreement (at least among archaeologists) that there was a measure of continuing life in towns and in some rural settlements into the fifth century, it would be surprising if so basic and easily supplied an amenity as domestic pottery expired suddenly and totally within a few years after 400. It is surely more likely that local and family potters continued to produce vessels and to distribute them over a limited area. One might thus expect to find vessels in fairly simple forms and in coarse fabrics on sites occupied at the end of the Roman period, this material representing the final phase of a disintegrating industry. In the Coritanian area at least, it must be admitted that such a state of affairs cannot be detected. In the latest stratified deposits which can be recognized[10] (dating from the final two decades of the fourth century) the industry still presents itself as a lively concern and it is hard to point to any vessels which might represent a do-it-yourself phase before the final extinction of the craft. It is equally hard to accept that the workshops active about 400 did not survive until at least the decade 410-20, and possibly somewhat later. Proof is unattainable, since at this period there are no artifacts which might be found in association with the pottery and which can provide a date for it. Coinage has by now dried up to a trickle and the few items of metalwork offer no real assistance.

If the potteries of early-fifth-century eastern Britain rapidly became moribund, leaving no appreciable influence on the wares of the later centuries, the same was not true of the Romano-British tradition of metalworking. Here it is possible to trace a clear thread of continuity between Roman Britain and Germanic England, not only in the well known hanging-bowls, but also in humbler and plainer bronze cauldrons and bowls, and in penannular brooches.

Although the hanging-bowls[11] will continue to provoke debate, it is widely agreed that technically and stylistically the earlier examples reveal the continuance of British crafts (and thus of British craftsmen) in the area first settled by the Anglo-Saxons. The earliest known representatives of the entire hanging-bowl series have turned up in the Coritanian area or on its northern fringes. Of the two bowls from Finningley, near Doncaster, claimed by Kendrick[12] as the earliest yet recorded, one has three escutcheons with little animal heads serving as hooks for the suspension-chains. These creatures resemble pre-Roman Celtic animals with their pronounced knobbed manes. Two plain escutcheons, probably from the same kind of early bowl, come from Twyford (Leics.),[13] possibly from a sixth-century cemetery. The Finningley and Twyford vessels are unlikely to date much after 400 and they may well be of the late fourth century.[14] Another early type of escutcheon, decorated with openwork peltas, has also been recorded in the area, at Eastwell (Leics.).[15] Lindsey can boast three or four fifth-century bowls, the earliest being those from Nettleton and Barton-on-Humber.[16] Some of the earliest bowls with enamelled escutcheons have also been found in the midlands, the best examples being the two Leicestershire specimens of Stoke Golding and Keythorpe,[17] and most handsome of all early hanging-bowls, that from Baginton.[18]

The hanging-bowls are the products of smiths who had a long tradition behind them. Other products of native bronze-smiths in the late Empire make it clear that this tradition was an extremely lively one. Its *pièce de resistance* is the unique bucket from Mount Sorrell in Charnwood Forest,

35. The bucket from Mount Sorrell (Leics.)

found in a well which appears to have been filled up about 300 or shortly afterwards (fig. 35).[19] The bucket is made up of a number of oak staves, bound top and bottom with sheet bronze and decorated by half-ovals of bronze, bearing raised discs with rivet-like bosses in their centres. The most startling features, however, are the two handle-attachments in the form of ox-heads. These are of impressively sombre creatures, their flat foreheads and long, narrow cheeks falling vertically away beneath the curving jut of the horns. These beasts lower back over a wasteland of three centuries of Roman provincial art towards oxen of the same breed which adorned buckets and tankards in the first century B.C. Other metalwork of the late Roman period is scarce but, in what we do possess, the British element is dominant.

Life in the towns of lowland Britain at this time probably resembled that of the cities of the Danubian provinces in the same period, so pathetically described by Eugippius in the *Vita Sancti Severini*. There the urban communities struggled on for several decades after the end of formal administration, before being engulfed one by one. The evidence for Lincoln and Leicester in the fifth century does not rival what is available for the final phase of Verulamium, Canterbury or Dorchester-on-Thames,[20] but at both places there is enough to indicate at least the continuance of life. In the case of Lincoln, moreover, the sum of the evidence suggests the survival of a community.

In both the upper and lower *colonia* at Lincoln, excavation has as yet revealed very little post-Roman material which is earlier than the tenth century A.D. Two early pagan Saxon vessels were formerly believed to have come from Lincoln but their exact provenance is not certain and they cannot be allowed into the argument with their present pedigree.[21] The absence of any trace of a large, early Anglo-Saxon cremation cemetery within ten miles of Lincoln (fig. 36) is striking and makes one wonder whether this does not indicate that the British inhabitants of *Lindum* and its surrounding territory held out during much or all of the fifth century without the aid of a federate garrison.[22] This is fragile evidence it is true, and liable to be shattered by a future discovery of a suitably early Germanic cemetery. But there is another tantalizing hint that the native Britons played some role in the politics of fifth century Lindsey. The third king in the Lindsey genealogy is one Caedbad, whose name contains the Celtic element *caed* (battle), and who presumably was at least partly of British stock.[23] This may be a case of a local chieftain, whose family had linked themselves with the immigrants by marriage but who still retained some influence in local affairs. The name of Caedbad is therefore instructive in suggesting one situation which could arise on the break-down of provincial authority. Not until the early seventh century, however, is there good evidence for an organized community at Lincoln. As Bede records,[24] in 627 Paulinus converted the Anglian Blaecca, who is described as *praefectus Lindocolinae civitatis*. It is not too optimistic to view this office as a possible remnant of the late Roman civic order, but it is difficult to foresee how this might be proved or disproved. We are turned back to excavation in Lincoln itself.

In contrast with Lincoln, Leicester is known to have a large cremation cemetery in its immediate environs, at Thurmaston, 4.8 km. north of the town on the Fosse Way. The earliest of these graves date from the middle of the fifth century.[25] Further, one early cremation urn has been reported from a spot immediately outside the Roman defences of *Ratae*, while another Anglo-Saxon cemetery of uncertain date lay at West Cotes. For the end of Roman buildings and institutions, however, we are no better off than in the case of Lincoln, and the results of recent excavation within the Roman walls do not encourage any hopes for a significant change in the situation. As at Lincoln, by the seventh century Leicester was certainly supporting a community. A bishop resided here about 680, although the See was not finally established until 737.

All too little is known about how the defence of towns was organized. There are two possible kinds of garrison: a militia drawn from the local inhabitants or a unit of soldiers, either from the regular army or from the forces of federate barbarian defenders upon which the British communities came increasingly to depend during the first half of the fifth century. Archaeologically, both kinds of unit appear to be detectable. Regular units of the army are represented by parts of uniform-fittings, especially buckles, belt-plates, strap-ends,[26] and the like. A few of these have been recorded in this region, at Leicester, *Margidunum*, and a number of open settlements. While there can be no doubt that many, or most, of the earlier types of these items of equipment were indeed military gear, issued by state factories in the frontier districts of the Rhine and Danube, it is dangerous to assume that *all* the metalwork of this kind was necessarily worn by soldiers. It would not be surprising if this striking new military gear stimulated a new fashion in civilian metalwork and, thus, occasional finds of it need signify no more than that a minor art-style was spreading among the civilian population.[27] The implications of the finds in towns of equipment (of which some items are specifically military) are nevertheless of major importance. Whether they signify more or less permanent garrisons or no more than line-of-communication troops is not clear.[28]

The earliest positive evidence of federate barbarians is a series of cremation cemeteries (in which the remains are contained in Anglo-Saxon urns) lying close to the walls of several towns in eastern England. Obviously, the burials of barbarians outside the Roman walls, *more Romano*, can be most reasonably explained as those of settlers who have been imported as federates to assist in the defence of still-lively Romano-British communities.[29] The most interesting concentration of early cemeteries in the Coritanian region lies about, and in, the Ancaster Gap. At Ancaster itself a series of fifth-century urn-burials has come from a cemetery immediately to the south of the Roman walls.[30] From the same spot, late Roman inhumation graves are also recorded. Only 8 km. away to the west is the huge urnfield of Loveden Hill, the earliest graves in which certainly date from the mid-fifth century.[31] Somewhat later cemeteries at nearby Carlton Scroop, Honington and Caythorpe demonstrate the perennial attractiveness of this area of light soil. Elsewhere in Lincolnshire, the fortified sites of Caistor and Horncastle both have early cemeteries close by, at Nettleton and Fonaby in the case of Caistor,[32] and perhaps at West Keal in the case of Horncastle.[33] Another Anglo-Saxon warrior-burial with sword and spear, which could well belong to the fifth

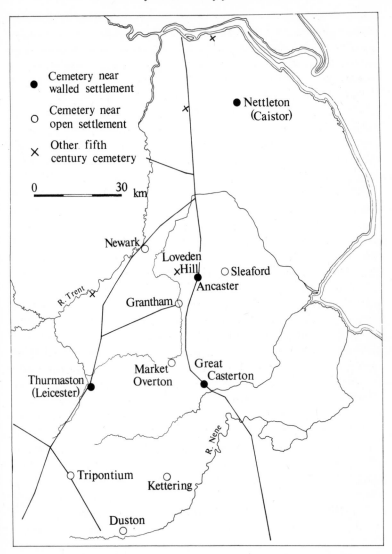

Cemetery near
walled settlement

Cemetery near
open settlement

Other fifth
century cemetery

0   30 km

● Nettleton
(Caistor)

Newark

Loveden
×Hill
Ancaster

○ Sleaford

R. Trent

Grantham

Thurmaston
(Leicester)

Market
Overton

Great
Casterton

R. Nene

Tripontium

Kettering

Duston

36. Fifth-century cemeteries in the territory of the Coritani

century, is recorded from Horncastle itself.[34] Further south,
at Great Casterton, Anglo-Saxon cremations and late Roman
inhumations lay hugger-mugger outside the north defences of
the settlement,[35] recalling the situation at Ancaster. On the

Fosse Way, one of the largest of all Anglo-Saxon cemeteries at Millgate, Newark,[36] is less than 800 metres from a Roman settlement known to have been occupied down to the late fourth century at least. The Newark urns go back to the middle of the fifth century, or even a little earlier. All this is a striking demonstration of continuity in one of the most important elements of the settlement-pattern. The occasional deviant from the general trend must be noted, e.g. the fifth- and early sixth-century cemetery at South Elkington, near Louth, perhaps representing a rather poor and isolated community.[37]

While towns (or at least some of them) certainly attracted Germanic settlers in the fifth century, it has long been apparent that by about 500, at the latest, the villa was a thing of the past. Several Coritanian villas have produced items of Anglo-Saxon pottery and metalwork, but none of these finds constitute evidence that early settlers moved into the villa buildings and continued their use. *Structural* evidence for post-Roman occupation of a villa site is so far limited to a group of seven post-holes dug into fourth-century floors in the Southwell house.[38] Probably associated with these was a sixth-century pot, which suggests that we are dealing with an occupation which had been resumed after a considerable break, a notion which receives support from the fact that there had been time for a deposit of soil to accumulate on the latest Roman floor before the timber structure went up.

None of the Anglo-Saxon material so far recovered from villas need indicate anything more than squatter occupations of relatively brief duration. The houses, then, did not survive under Anglo-Saxon masters. But what of the estates of which they were the centres? About this major subject, archaeology has nothing to say at present. It is not unlikely, however, that some estates were taken over in their entirety and farmed by the new settlers, who chose new sites for their dwellings. It was precisely the agriculturally rewarding land which the villas were exploiting that the Anglo-Saxons sought to take over, and thus the pattern of early Anglo-Saxon land-colonisation *may* be more closely related to the villa-estates than is generally acknowledged. There are formidable difficulties in the way of anyone trying to demonstrate continuity between the economic arrangements of Romano-British landowners and Anglo-Saxon settlers. The most determined attempt so far made, that of Professor Finberg,[39] has proved more acceptable to historians than to archaeologists, but his thesis should not be over-hastily discarded. Rather, it should be tested in an area of *primary* Anglo-Saxon settlement, where the newcomers are likelier to have encountered estates in their late Roman forms, and in which entire land-units might have been assigned to federate bands. Beyond these expressions of hope we cannot at present go: beyond this (as the old cartographer wisely wrote) there are monsters. But as detailed field-surveys of limited areas gradually become available, fresh approaches toward a solution of one of the major problems of early English history will be possible. But since this is indeed an English problem, we must here take leave of the Coritani.

Notes and references

References to British journals use the abbreviations recommended by the Council for British Archaeology, which are those of the American Standards Association (list Z39, 5-1963 (revised 1966). Other abbreviations used are:

BRGK   *Bericht der Römisch-Germanischen Kommission*
CIL   *Corpus Inscriptionum Latinarum*
PW   Pauly-Wissowa-Kroll, *Realencyclopaedie der klassischen Altertumswissenschaft*
RIB   R.G. Collingwood and R.P. Wright *Roman Inscriptions of Britain* i (Oxford 1965)
VCH   *Victoria County History*

1. TRIBAL TERRITORY AND THE PRE-ROMAN IRON AGE

1. Allen *1961* and *1963*.
2. Allen *1963*, 22ff.
3. Kenyon *1948*, 124ff.
4. Report by C.F.C. Hawkes forthcoming in *Trans. Leicester Archaeol. Soc.*
5. Ancaster: recent excavations by the Univ. of Nottingham, the first report on which will appear shortly. Old Sleaford: unpublished excavation by Mrs M.U. Jones for the Dept. of the Environment. *J. Roman Stud.* 1i (1961), 171; 1ii (1962), 167.
6. Excavation still continuing. Interim report, May *1970*.
7. Kirmington: *Lincolnshire Hist. Archaeol.* i (1966), 43. *E. Midland Archaeol. Bull.* viii (1965), 9f. Owmby: *Lincolnshire Hist. Archaeol.* i (1966), 44f. ix (1966),7. S. Ferriby: Hawkes, S.C. *1963*.
8. S. Ferriby: *Numis. Chron.* 1908, 17ff. (Other coin-finds in *Brit Numis. J.* iii (1906), 1ff., Grimsby (Scartho): *Numis. Chron.* 1947, 65ff.; 1955, 243.

9. above, p. 107.
10. W.F. Grimes in Frere *1961*, 23f. Cf. also the enclosed settlement at Draughton (Northants.), *op. cit.* 21f.
11. Swinnerton *1932*, 239ff. Baker *1960*, 31ff.
12. Kenyon *1950*, 17ff. *Antiq. J.* xliv (1964)), 122ff.
13. Allen *1963* provides the essential basis for this section.
14. Such as are recorded in Gaul: Caesar, *De Bello Gallico* i, 16, 6 (Divitiacus and Liscus among the Aedui), and the coin of the Lexovii with the legend CISIAMBOS CATTOS VERGOBRETO.
15. Allen *1970*, 15f.
16. *Primitive Government* (1962), 14.
1.7. Tacitus, *Annales* ii, 20, referring to a boundary earthwork between the Cherusci and the Angrivarii. On rivers as tribal boundaries, R. von Scheliha, *Die Wassergrenze im Altertum* (Breslau 1931).
18. This is not necessarily true, however, of all Iron Age coinages. Allen *1970*, 11 on Icenian coins which appear to bear an abbreviation of the tribal name.
19. Allen *1963*, 13ff.
20. The edition of C. Muller, (Paris 1883 & 1901) covers Books I-V and has a parallel Latin translation. The section on Britain is in Book II. A complete text is provided in Nobbe's edition of 1843-5 (repr. in 1966).
21. Rivet *1964*, 132.
22. Colley Weston: *Archaeol. J.* cxxii (1965), 52ff. Brigstock: *Antiq. J.* xliii (1963), 228ff.
23. Rivet *1964*, 134. Note that this is likely to apply in a pre-Roman organization rather than in a Roman province.
24. Foster & Alcock *1963*, 242. Richmond assigned Wall to the Coritani, but this is to draw the boundary too far to the west.
25. *Geographia* ii, 3, 10. Richmond, *The Geography of Brigantia* in Wheeler, *The Earthworks at Stanwick*, Research Report no. XVII of the Society of Antiquaries of London (1954), 61f.
26. For fresh information on the chronology of Roman garrisons in Derbyshire: *Derbyshire Archaeol. J.* lxxxi (1961), 108 f.; lxxxvii (1967), 70ff. (Little Chester). lxxxvii (1967), 99ff.; lxxxviii (1968), 154ff.; lxxxix (1969), 89ff. and lxc (1970), 99ff. (Brough-on-Noe)
27. On the British section of this document, Rivet *1970*.
28. Crawford & Richmond *1949*.
29. *J. Roman Stud.* xxx (1940), 190. The stamps of CVNOARD or CVNOARDA are unpublished.
30. e.g. *RIB* 250; *CIL* VIII, 21669; XIII, 6679.
31. *Causennae* was moved about the map freely in the eighteenth century. Since the later nineteenth, Ancaster has been the accepted identification, and this was the choice of the compilers of the third edition of the Ordnance Survey Map of Roman Britain (1956). Rivet *1970*, 48 points out the difficulties involved in accepting this. Since it is not clear which route is being followed in the

Itinerary, the precise location of *Causennae* will probably never be certain. There are three candidates: Sapperton (on King Street), Threekingham (on Mareham Lane) and Blue Harbour Junction (on Ermine Street).

32. This was first attested as a major settlement by excavation in the early years of the twentieth century: *VCH Notts.* ii, 12ff. There has been no recent excavation. Informative air photographs are provided by Dr St. Joseph in Wacher *1966*, 27f.

33. *ibid.* and *Trans. Thoroton Soc. Nottinghamshire* xlii (1938), 1ff.; lxix (1965), 19ff. Older suggestions that *Ad Pontem* derived its name from a bridge carrying the Fosse Way over marshy ground near the Trent bank must be discounted. The bridge must surely have been over the Trent itself, carrying a road leading north-west along the Greet valley.

34. Todd *1969* (with refs. to earlier publications).

35. K.H. Jackson in Rivet *1970*, 80.

36. Identification of these two places is now secure. High Cross: Greenfield & Webster *1955*. Churchover: Cameron & Lucas *1967*.

37. Crawford & Richmond *1949*, 24.

38. *op. cit.* 23. cf. DEA ARNOMECTA at Brough-on-Noe: *RIB* 281.

39. *VCH Derbyshire* i, 222ff. This must lie outside the tribal area.

40. cf. Malton on the Yorkshire Derwent, Rivet *1970*, 72.

41. *Derbyshire Archaeol. J.* lxxx (1960), 78f.

42. Rocester: Webster *1962*. Chesterton: *VCH Staffs.* i, 189. *N. Staffordshire J. Field Stud.* i (1961), 26ff. *Britannia* i (1970), 190 records the discovery of a fort here.

43. Cameron *1959*, ii, 231.

2. HISTORY: A.D. 43-367

1. Recent studies of this period are: Dudley and Webster *1965*, Frere *1967*, 61ff, and Webster *1970*.

2. Todd *1968a*, 38.

3. Allen *1944*, 19ff.; Frere *1967*, 41ff.

4. Holme: *J. Roman Stud.* li (1961), 120. Newton: *J. Roman Stud.* lv (1965), 75f.; lix (1969). Part of one side only is so far known. It includes a gate with *clavicula*.

5. *J. Roman Stud.* lv (1965), 75f.

6. *J. Roman Stud.* lviii (1968), 190 fig. 13: lix (1969), 219. *Britannia* i (1970), 287.

7. A third large fort, of 9.3 ha., is now known at Rossington Bridge (Yorks.) *J. Roman Stud.* lix (1969), 103 and pl. ii (1). *Britannia* i (1970), 287. See above, p. 31.

8. *Antiquity* xiii (1939), 178ff. This fort is unexcavated, but the air photographs suggest that several periods of occupation are represented.

9. Todd *1968a*, 15ff.

10. *J. Roman Stud.* 1vi (1966), 203. *Britannia* i (1970), 284.
11. Frere *1967*, 71 n. 2, suggesting the Westgate area, perhaps beneath the medieval castle. Webster *1970*, 184 puts forward the South Common, south of the river Witham.
12. Todd *1968a*, pl. 1.
13. *op. cit.* 36f.
14. *op. cit.* 39 and 47.
15. Mellor *1969*, 6 and above, p. 55.
16. *J. Roman Stud.* 1iv (1964), 160 fig. 12; 1vi (1966), 204 fig. 10. Further information from the excavator, J.S. Wacher.
17. Webster *1970*, 194f. Excavation in 1970-1, by Mrs K.F. Hartley, revealed a length of a ditch of military pattern.
18. Todd *1969a*, 41 n. 4.
19. Toynbee *1964* 297 and pl. lxvi, 6. Clear air photographs of the site have produced no evidence for a fort as yet: St. Joseph in Wacher *1966*, 27f. The pottery from Brough in Newark Museum includes very little first century material, and nothing which is earlier than about 70.
20. A few Claudian coins have been reported from here, but no other evidence has been forthcoming. Walter *1908*, 4.
21. Webster *1970*, 184, and information from the excavator Miss E. Blank.
22. Whitwell *1970*, 17ff, summarizing the important information. *J. Roman Stud.* xxxix (1949), 57ff; xlvi (1956), 22ff; *Archaeol. J.* 1xvii (1960), 40ff. are the only fully published accounts.
23. *Northern Hist.* i (1966), 10. Frere *1967*, 70.
24. This can be explained by the fact that in Upper Germany, at least, turf useful for rampart construction is less freely available than in Britain, whereas timber is superabundant.
25. Oswald, F. *1941* and *1948* give the fullest accounts of his views.
26. Todd *1969a*, 42ff.
27. Oswald, F. *1952*, pl. ii and Todd *1969a*, 21ff.
28. *op cit.* 28f.
29. Hind, *The Broxtowe (Nottm.) Early Iron Age Settlement* (1940). (The fact that all the finds were Roman did not induce the author to alter this title.) *Third Annual Report of the Excavation Section of the Thoroton Society of Notts.* (1939), 6ff. *E. Midland Archaeol. Bull.* viii (1965), 30.
30. By Mr D.F. Mackreth.
31. *Derbyshire Archaeol. J.* 1xxxvii (1967), 162. Further information from Mr M. Brassington.
32. *J. Roman Stud.* xliii (1953), 87.
33. *Derbyshire Archaeol. J.* lxxxvii (1967), 165ff. Although this work might be Roman, its general similarity to certain seventeenth century earthworks should be noted: e.g. *RCHM Newark Civil War Earthworks* (1964), 38, fig. 7.
34. *Iter.Brit.* 96. *Brit.Rom.* 434. By 1723 the earthwork was no longer visible. On later observations here, *VCH Notts.* ii (1910), 19ff.

Unpublished excavations by J. Wade in 1968-70 revealed nothing earlier than about A.D. 70.

35. May, T. *1922*, pl. xxii. Simpson *1964*, 11 and fig. 1.
36. *J. Roman Stud.* lix (1969), 103 and pl. ii, 1. Another fort site is suspected at Robin Hood's Well, 6 miles NW of Doncaster on the road to Tadcaster.
37. *J. Roman Stud.* lv (1965), 205; lvi (1966), 202.
38. Todd *1968a*, 39.
39. Brough: *Derbyshire Archaeol. J.* lxxxvii (1967), 99; lxxxviii (1968), 154; lxxxix (1969), 89; lxc (1970), 99. Doncaster: recent excavations unpublished. Buxton: *VCH Derbyshire* i (1905), 222ff.
40. *Derbyshire Archaeol. J.* lxxxi (1961), 103 and 108ff.
41. *ibid.* lxxxi (1961), 108f.
42. On the inscription which provides the basis for this statement (*CIL* XIII, 6679), Richmond *1946a*, 29.
43. cf. Tacitus, *Annales* xiv, 27 for a not dissimilar case.
44. *RIB* 2241, dating from the reign of Victorinus (A.D. 268-70).
45. Richmond *1946b*, 65. For a recent account of all aspects of *Lindum Colonia*, Whitwell *1970*, 25ff.
46. Petch *1960*, 51.
47. Mellor *1969*, 3ff.
48. *Margidunum*: Todd *1969*, 49. Thorpe: *J. Roman Stud.* lvi (1966), 204 fig. 10.
49. Corder *1951*, 6ff. A close look at the published section-drawing, however, (fig. 3), suggests that the lowest layer of the rampart extends *beneath* the wall and that therefore the wall has been added to a pre-existing earthwork defence.
50. Corder *1951*, 14; *1954*, 3.
51. *J. Roman Stud.* liv (1964), 158 fig. 11 and Todd, forthcoming. There is no evidence here that the wall has been added to an earlier earthwork; wall and rampart are taken to be contemporary.
52. Wacher *1966*, 62ff. It has also been argued that wall and bank were contemporary and that both date from the late third or early fourth century. *Trans. Birmingham Warwickshire Archaeol. Soc.* lxxxiv (1967-70), 21.
53. St. Joseph in Wacher *1966*, 27ff.
54. It is unlikely that this question will ever be settled. For a recent debate: *J. Roman Stud.* lvi (1966), 92ff; lvii (1967), 61ff.
55. *J. Roman Stud.* xi (1921), 102. On the administration of Roman Britain in general, Frere *1967*, 191ff.
56. *Antiquity* xxxv (1961), 218f.
57. *Engl. Hist. Rev.* lii (1937), 199f.
58. *J. Roman Stud.* lvi (1966), 223.
59. Frere *1967*, 206.
60. Lincoln: *RIB* 2240 (Valerian A.D. 253-9), and *RIB* 2241 (Victorinus. A.D. 268-70). *Durobrivae*: *RIB* 2238 (Victorinus).
61. *RIB* 2242.

62. The best recent account of these sites and their history is contained in Cunliffe *1968*, 255ff. White *1961* is a study of the historical sources, which largely ignores the archaeological evidence.

63. Caistor: Hawkes *1946*, 23ff. and Rahtz *1960*, with references; recent work and observation is unpublished. Horncastle: Hawkes *1946*, 22f.; recent excavation is unpublished. On both sites, Whitwell *1970*, 69ff.

64. Described in Rahtz *1960*, 182ff.

65. Owen *1952*, 330ff.

66. *Itin.* (ed. L. Toulmin-Smith) iv, 181.

67. Owen, *1952*. 339

68. The Thames estuary approaches were covered by Reculver (Kent), the Wash by Brancaster (Norfolk). Reculver has produced an inscription attesting military occupation of the site in the early third century (*Antiq. J.* xli (1961), 224ff.), and the defences of Brancaster incorporate some structural elements which would be out of place after about the middle of the century. *Antiq. J.* xvi (1936), pl. lxxxiv opp. p. 450. Against the suggestion that the coastal forts extended southwards to the Humber, there is the fact that in the *Notitia Dignitatum* Brancaster is the most northerly fort.

69. e.g. Scampton (Lincs.): Illingworth *1808*, 7.

70. Oswald A. *1937*, 158. Elsewhere in this villa, however, *parts* of human skeletons were found (*op.cit.* 156f.), this being more consonant with destruction by an enemy.

3. COMMUNICATIONS AND URBAN SETTLEMENT

1. The dimensions of the ditch in its present state vary considerably: at Peterborough Within parish, 7.6-10.7 m. wide and about 3 m. deep; at another place in the same parish, 10.7-12.2 m. wide and 1.8-2.10 m. deep; at Werrington, about 15 metres wide; further north in the best preserved sectors, the ditch-hollow measures between 4.6 and 7.6 m. A berm is not invariably present.

2. Clark *1949*, 145ff.

3. Car Dyke: Trollope *1872*, 64ff.; King-Fane *1931*, 91f. Foss Dyke: Oswald, A, *1937a*, 13; Phillips *1935*, 117; Toynbee *1962*, 131.

4. King-Fane *1931*, 90f.

5. John Morton, *Natural History of Northamptonshire* (1712).

6. Hallam in Phillips *1970*, 63f.

7. That of Trollope *1872*, a still useful survey, though his profiles of the Dyke appear to be exaggerated.

8. On the sector immediately north of Peterborough, *RCHM Peterborough New Town* (1969), 40ff.

9. On these, Hallam in Phillips *1970*, 35. Other artificial channels in the Fenland which may be of Roman origin include the Asen Dyke, from the Welland to Aswick Grange, and the Westlode,

leading into Spalding from the west.

10. Trollope *1872*, 77f. Stukeley claimed that the Dyke had been defended by forts at Eye, Narborough, Billinghay, Walcot and elsewhere. He gave no supporting evidence for these sites and they appear to have been picked out at random.

11. An earlier surmise of mine, Todd *1966*, 145ff., was based on a mis-dating of the Timberland (Lincs.) coin-hoard.

12. Clark *1949*, 151ff.

13. Hallam in Phillips *1970*, 43ff.

14. e.g. Richmond *1963a*, 129. It will be remembered that Roman canals frequently formed part of drainage schemes: e.g. in the Pomptine marshes, *PW* Supp. viii, 1135ff.

15. Kenyon *1948*, 40f. The suggestion that it was an aqueduct is the least likely of all possible interpretations. Its form was not customary for a Roman aqueduct and in any case water could more easily be brought into *Ratae* from the north than from the south.

16. Frere *1967*, 245 suggests that it may have led to docks. But the natural place for docks would be on the Soar bank on the western side of the town, not on the south side towards which the Raw Dykes tend.

17. The archaeological sources for Leicester leave much to be desired. The town was not well served by nineteenth century antiquarians. Haverfield did what he could with the records of earlier finds in a characteristically sensible paper (Haverfield *1918*), but not even he could transmute much of the dross into gold. The principal results of Dr Kenyon's excavations of 1936-9 are discussed above (p. 59ff.). Much of the excavation carried out between 1945 and the present is unpublished, though the important discoveries are treated in the summaries in *Trans. Leicester Archaeol. Soc.* Mellor *1969* is a useful account of the major results achieved in 1965-9. A report on the excavations of the forum by M. Hebditch and Miss J. E. Mellor will appear shortly.

18. Kenyon *1948*, 9f and 125ff.

19. C.F.C. Hawkes in *Trans. Leicester Archaeol. Soc.* forthcoming.

20. Webster *1958*, 84 for the belt-plate and eagle terminal; the pommel and scabbard-hook appear to be unpublished. All in Leicester Mus.

21. *J. Roman Stud.* lviii (1968), 186. Mellor *1969*, 6 and pl.ii.

22. Excavated by Mr J. S. Wacher in 1958.

23. Haverfield *1918*, 26 and pl. v, a.

24. Kenyon *1948*, 14ff. and above, p. 59.

25. Mellor *1969*, 1ff.

26. Mellor forthcoming. Frere *1967*, 204, written before study of the material from recent excavations, suggested that the forum may be pre-Flavian. This is now clearly untrue.

27. *Trans. Leicester Archaeol. Soc.* xxxv (1959), 79f. and *J. Roman Stud.* xlix (1959), 113ff. with fig. 10.

28. *Saalburg Jahrbuch* ix (1939), 6ff.

29. Kenyon *1948*, 28ff.

.30. It is not clear whether this was roofed or not.

31. *Trans. Leicester Archaeol. Soc.* xxxv (1959), 78.

32. Mellor *1969*, 6.

33. Kenyon *1948*, 38ff. *Trans. Leicester Archaeol. Soc.* xxxv (1959), 80.

34. *Britannia* i (1970), 286.

35. Leicester Mus.

36. *RIB* 244

37. *Trans. Leicester Archaeol. Soc.* xxxv (1959), 78f.

38. Mellor *1969*, 8, with pls. ib and iii

39. Toynbee *1964*, 236.

40. *op. cit.* 279.

41. This is probably a second-century floor. Some of the red tesserae in it have proved to be fragments of Antonine samian bowls: identified by Mr B.R. Hartley.

42. Toynbee *1964*, 279. *1962*, pl. 219.

43. Pottery kilns in High Street: Haverfield *1918*, 43. The large quantity of ox-heads found by Mr Wacher in the remains of the house off Blue Boar Lane may well be the result of preparations for tanning: *Trans. Leicester Archaeol. Soc.* xxxv (1959), 79.

44. Haverfield *1918*, 24.   VERECVNDA
                               LVDIA LVC
                               IVS GLADIA
                               TOR

45. Haverfield *1918*, 44; *VCH Leics.* i (1907), 196f.

46 Their problems are briefly surveyed in Todd *1970*.

47. Todd *1969a* (with refs.).

48. Corder *1961*, 11ff.

49. *op.cit.* 33ff.

50. Ancaster: *E. Midland Archaeol. Bull.* ix (1966), 11, fig. 2. Old Sleaford: *J. Roman Stud.* li (1961), 171; lii (1962), 167.

51. May *1970*, 232.

52. Navenby: *E. Midland Archaeol. Bull.* viii (1965), 18, fig. 5. Foston: Whitwell *1970*, 76f.

4. RURAL SETTLEMENT

1. RCHM *A Matter of Time* (London 1960), Webster & Hobley *1964*, Simpson W.G. *1966*.

2. This is particularly true of the Vale of Belvoir and the Keuper Marl area of Nottinghamshire.

3. The maps are based with modifications, on those of Darby, H.C., & Terrett, I.B., *The Domesday Geography of Midland England* (Cambridge 1954) and Darby, H.C., & Maxwell, I.S., *The Domesday Geography of Northern England* (Cambridge 1962).

4. The map shows very few Roman settlements in this area. This most

probably reflects the lack of extensive field-work rather than the true state of affairs.

5. I am indebted to Mr J. Pickering for information about this region, derived from his air photographs.

6. But this part of the Fenland has still not been studied as carefully as the areas further south.

7. e.g. Richmond in Rivet *1969*, 49ff. and Smith, J.T. *1963*.

8. The most informative sites are unpublished in full: e.g. Great Casterton, Corder *1951*, 15ff.; *1954*, 11ff.; *1961*, 59ff. Great Weldon, *J. Roman Stud.* xliv (1954), 95 fig. 15; xlvi (1956), 131 fig. 32. Important results have been accumulating in the continuing programme of work at Winterton: interim report, Stead *1966*.

9. Norfolk Street: *VCH Leics.* i (1907), 196; Haverfield *1918*, 44 Southwell: Daniels *1966*. Scampton: Illingworth *1808*.

10. D.J. Smith in Daniels *1966*, 33ff.

11. This wall-plaster is unpublished. A reconstruction hangs in the south transept of Southwell Minster.

12. Inhumation burials found in the remains of the building *may* be associated with the nearby chapel of St. Pancras.

13. Rooke *1787*. Oswald, A. *1949*.

14. Notably those in Scarcliffe Park Wood: *Britannia* i (1970), 284.

15. Oswald, A. *1949*, 2ff.

16. *op. cit.* plan 1.

17. Kay *1956*.

18. In the Museum of the University of Nottingham.

19. *Vetusta Monumenta* ii (1789), pl. ix. Stead *1966*. Wm. Fowler, *Coloured Engravings* . . . (1804). Information about this villa has been greatly increased by the recent work of Mr R. Goodburn. Among the latest discoveries are animal pounds. For rectangular enclosures close to the villa, see above, p. 90ff.

20. *Bedfords. Archaeol. J.* v (1970), 57.

21. Denton: Smith, J.T. *1964*. Empingham: unpublished excavation by the late M.J. Dean and M.S. Gorin in 1969-71.

22. Report by E. Greenfield forthcoming in *Lincolnshire Hist. Archaeol.*

23., Frere *1967*, 271.

24. It is worth noting that one of these, Oakley (Northants.) was *replaced* by a stone round-house during the second century. *J. Roman Stud.* lvi (1966), 207; lvii (1967), 186.

25. Oswald A. *1937*, 140 and figs. 1 & 2. The bulk of this material appears to be Flavian and nothing need be earlier than about A.D. 60.

26. Lockleys: *Antiq. J.* xviii (1938), 344ff. Park Street: *Archaeol. J.* cii (1945), 25f.

27. Corder *1961*, 59ff.

28. Cromwell: revealed by air photographs taken by Dr St. Joseph (fig. 21). Winterton: (fig. 22), air photograph taken by Mr D.N. Riley in 1971.

29. Information from Dr D.J. Smith.

30. Corder *1961*, 70f. Another close-set pair of walls with no clear function occurs at Empingham, 6.5 km. away.

31. Rivet *1969*, 216.

32. Simpson, W.G. *1966*, 15ff.

33. Simpson, W.G. *1966*, 20, fig. 4.

34. An extensive coverage has been assembled by the Trent Valley Archaeological Research Committee, and these are housed in the Museum of the University of Nottingham.

35. Breaston: excavated by D.A. Reaney in 1967. Willington: excavated by Miss H. Wheeler in 1971-2. Rampton: excavated by M. Ponsford in 1966; brief notice in *E. Midlands Archaeol. Bull.* ix (1966), 41.

36. *Antiquity* xlii (1968), 46f.

37. Excavated by the writer in 1970.

38. Edlington Wood: Corder *1951b*. Scarcliffe: excavated by H.C. Lane; brief notice in *Britannia* i (1970), 284. Scratta Wood: excavated by the Worksop Arch. Soc.

39. *VCH Derbyshire* i (1905), 233ff. Further information from the late Mr J. Radley.

40. Colley Weston: Knocker *1965*. Brigstock: Greenfield *1963*.

41. *Antiq. J.* xliii (1963), 264ff.

42. Excavated by Mr E. Greenfield., Lewis *1966*, 84 & 93ff, pl. iv.

43. Excavated by Mr E. Greenfield. The curse tablet: *J. Roman Stud.* liii (1963), 122.

44. Both of these were found in the same year: *J. Roman. Stud.* xlii (1962), 192.

Ancaster:	Nettleham:
DEO VIRIDIO	DEO MARTI RIGO
TRENICO ARCVM	NEMETI ET NUMINI
FECIT DE SVO DON	BVS AVGVSTORVM
	Q NERAT PROXSI
	MVS ARCVM DE SVO
	DONAVIT

45. *Antiq. J.* xliii (1963), 292.

46. In University of Nottingham: unpublished.

47. *Lincolnshire Hist. Archaeol.* i (1966), 43.

5. INDUSTRY AND THE ECONOMY

1. In this region one can cite the evidence from *Margidunum* and Thorpe (above, p. 29ff.).

2. above, p. 6.

3. These are areas where extensive modern mining has been responsible for the discovery of many ancient sites. The incidence of sites in the distribution pattern is thus disproportionately high in these districts.

4. Tylecote *1962*, 217ff.
5. Corder *1961*, 36f. and 84f.
6. Dudley *1949*, 194ff. Other north Lincolnshire sites are noted in Whitwell *1970*, 113.
7. *Norfolk Archaeol.* xxxii (1960), 142ff.
8. *J. Roman Stud.* lii (1962), 173. Tylecote *1970*, 24f., figs. 2 & 3. Their date falls in the early second century.
9. Hannah *1932*, 262ff. Tylecote *1962*, 230f.
10. *J. Roman Stud.* xvi (1926), 223; xix (1929), 193; xxx (1940), 169; xlv (1955), 89. This is often termed a villa, but in truth its character is not clear. Tylecote *1970*, 24 asserts that the bloomery was inserted into the building in the late-Roman or post-Roman period.
11. *J. Roman Stud.* lvi (1966), 207. Roasting the ore was intended to remove as much useless matter as possible before smelting.
12. *Trans. Leicester Archaeol. Soc.* xxxii (1956), 17ff.
13. A cautionary note must be sounded here. It is clear from several sites that iron ore could be roasted and then transported far from its source to be smelted. Much more work is required on the actual sources of the ore. There are at least three possible sources: the ironstone beds, the deposits of bog-iron, and nodules of ironstone in the river-gravel.
14. *J. Roman Stud.* li (1961), 176 fig. 22.
15. This idea has been suggested by several writers: Hawkes in Dudley *1949*, 218: Whitwell *1970*, 88.
16. Tylecote *1962*, 225.
17. *Bull. Loughborough Archaeol. Soc.* v (1962), 15.
18. This branch of the industry deserves more attention than it has yet received.
19. *Antiquity* xi (1937), 143ff.; xv (1941), 16ff. *Trans. Leicester Archaeol. Soc.* xxvi (1950), 75ff.
20. For a recent discussion of the localities in which granite and 'slate' occur, Sylvester-Bradley and Ford *1968*, 47ff.
21. *RCHM Roman London* (1928), 157 and pl. 57 (carved sarcophagus).
22. Icklingham: Clark, *East Anglia* (1960), 126. Arbury Road: *Proc. Cambridgeshire Antiq. Soc.* xlix (1955), 17.
23. Godmanchester: *Archaeol. News Letter* vii (1960), 256. Lord's Bridge, near Cambridge: Fox *1926*, 194.
24. Wheeler *1936*, 142.
25. Liversidge in Steers *1965*, 129.
26. Except for the milestone of Ancaster stone set up in the centre of Lincoln (*RIB* 2241).
27. Frere *1967*, 288.
28. Kenyon *1948*, 14 and Leicester Mus. records.
29. *loc. cit.*
30. Todd *1969a*, 82.
31. Richmond *1946b*, 54.

32. *Trans. Leicester Archaeol. Soc.* xviii (1934-5), 185f.

33. Toynbee *1964*, 48f.

34. *Archaeologia* xxxii (1847), 13ff.; *VCH Hunts.* i (1926), 226f.

35. *ibid.* Toynbee *1962*, no. 27 and pl. 26 (Minerva).

36. Trollope *1870*, 8f. Frere *1961*, 230f.

37. *Rep. Pap. Lincolnshire Archit. Archaeol. Soc.* x (1963-4), 62 and pl. 3.

38. Lincoln Mus., unpublished.

39. *VCH Notts.* ii (1910), 24 and fig. 7.

40. Hallam *1960*, 35ff.

41. Swinnerton *1932*, 239ff.

42. *Digest* 48, 19, 8.

43. Solinus, *Coll. rerum memorabilium* (ed. Mommsen 1895), 102, is probably to be taken to indicate that Romano-British coal was used at the temple of Sul Minerva at Bath.

44. Webster *1955*, 201f.

45. Excavation in the past fifteen years has greatly enlarged our knowledge of this industrial centre. This work is not yet published. Brief account in Hartley *1960*.

46. Recent excavations here too have been very informative. *J. Roman Stud.* lv (1965), 208; lvi (1966), 206.

47. *Lincolnshire Hist. Archaeol.* i (1966), 40f.

48. Gillam *1939*, 429ff. Revised dates are suggested in Todd *1968b*, 202, and Jones and Webster *1969*, 18ff. A start about 120 now seems likely after excavation of kilns at Little Chester. *Antiq. J.* li (1971), 43f.

49. Longthorpe and Ancaster are unpublished. Great Casterton: Todd *1968a*, 42ff. Since this was written, kilns producing fine wares, destined for use by the garrison, have been found outside the Longthorpe fortress.

50. Woods *1969*, 3ff.

51. That is, there is no indication as yet of the activity of a military works depot, like the early second century example at Holt (Denbighs.).

52. Corder and Bunch *1954*, 218ff.

53. Publication by Dr D. J. Smith and the writer forthcoming. The concentration of mid and late first century kilns about the upper Nene valley is a remarkable phenomenon which at present cannot be satisfactorily explained.

54. Todd *1968c*, 38ff.

55. Dragonby: *E. Midland Archaeol. Bull.* vii (1964), 7 fig. 2. Lea: *J. Roman Stud.* xlviii (1958), 136. North Hykeham: Thompson *1958*, 15ff.

56. Wasters in Leicester Mus.

57. Todd *1969b*, 382ff.

58. Great Casterton: Corder *1961*, 50f. South Carlton: Webster *1944*, 129ff.

59. Cantley: Annable *1960. Yorkshire Archaeol. Soc.* cli (1954), 403,

407, 538; cliii (1956), 32; cliv (1957), 364. Rossington Bridge: unpublished. Material in Doncaster Mus.

60. Recent unpublished work by Mrs K.F. Hartley.
61. above, p. 120.
62. On Dales Ware: Gillam *1951*, 154ff. On both types: Todd *1968b*, 202ff.
63. Todd *1968b*, 192ff.
64. It now seems likely that Lincoln was a major centre of the production of these wares.
65. The dating of this important kiln-complex is not yet settled. A start about 325 seems probable. Nineteenth-century discoveries at nearby Boultham suggest that more kilns remain to be found.
66. For instance, the *wheel-made* Anglo-Saxon vessel from the Anglo-Saxon cemetery at Newark. The so-called 'Romano-Saxon' vessels are also often termed hybrids. These pots bear stamped and/or bossed ornament, arranged in a way which recalls that of early Anglo-Saxon wares. The vessels themselves, however, are in usual Romano-British fabrics and are wheel-turned. It has been argued (Myres *1956*, 34ff.) that they are products of Romano-British potters aiming at a market among Germanic immigrants of the fourth century. Probably the significance of these vessels has been over-emphasized. It is not certain that the 'Romano-Saxon' ornament actually is German-inspired. It may equally well belong to the repertoire of Romano-British potters. Moreover, some of the vessels appear to be too early to have anything to do with Germanic settlers.

6. THE LATE FOURTH AND FIFTH CENTURIES

1. This programme of restoration was carried through by Count Theodosius in and after 370, on his recovery of the provinces from barbarian hands. Frere, *1967*, 256 & 357.
2. Elslack: *Yorkshire Archaeol. J.* xxi (1911), 113ff. Newton Kyme: *J. Roman Stud.* xlvii (1957), 209.
3. above, p. 42ff.
4. Corder *1961*, 27ff. It is now generally agreed that the date of about 355-60 suggested by Corder is too early. More probably these modifications to town defences formed part of the Theodosian programme after 367-9. Following Corder *1955*, most writers on Roman Britain have accepted that the towers were designed to house artillery. This is open to question.
5. *J. Roman Stud.* lv (1965), 206 fig. 12 (SW angle). Todd, forthcoming (NW angle). These towers have no parallels in Roman Britain. They are, however, close to late fourth century towers in certain of the Pannonian forts: e.g. Transaquincum, *Budapest Regiseigi* xiv (1945), 489f.; Campona, S.Paulovics, *Il Limes romano in Ungheria* (1938), 12ff. The apparition of a Danubian tower-type

at Ancaster can be best explained as a result of the transfer to the site either of a military engineer or an army unit in the period after 369.

6. above, p. 61.
7. *Trans. Thoroton Soc. Nottinghamshire* 1xii (1958), 24ff.
8. It may be compared in its function to the fortlets on the Cologne-Bavai road: Mertens & Leva *1966*, 1064ff.
9. Great Casterton: Corder *1961*, 63ff. Denton: Smith J.T. *1964*, 86 and 90. Unpublished information about Great Weldon from Dr D.J. Smith.
10. e.g. in the destruction deposit of the Great Casterton villa: Corder *1951*, 24ff.
11. The most useful works on these are: Kendrick *1932*, Kilbride-Jones *1936*, Henry *1955*, Haseloff *1958*, and Fowler *1968*.
12. Kendrick *1932*, 165.
13. Hawkes in Grimes *1951*, 198, pl. ix, 3, 4, 5.
14. The Finningley specimens were dated to the early fourth century by Kilbride-Jones *1936*, 212. This is about a century too early.
15. *Medieval Archaeol.* viii (1964), pl. xix, c and d.
16. Nettleton: *Archaeol. J.* ciii (1946), 89. Barton-on-Humber: *loc. cit.* Dudley *1949*, 228f.
17. Stoke Golding: Kilbride-Jones *1936*, fig. 8/2, 3. Keythorpe: now lost. *Archaeol. J.* xvii (1861), 76.
18. Henry *1936*, pl. 25/1.
19. *Proc. Cambridgeshire Antiq. Soc.* viii (1892-3), 133ff. Hawkes *1951*, 197f.
20. Frere in Wacher *1966*, 87ff. Frere *1967*, 375ff.
21. Myres *1951b*, 98.
22. Dr Myres long ago wondered along these lines (Collingwood and Myres *1936*, 414) and then allowed the above-mentioned Saxon vessels to change his mind. See now Myres *1969*, 76.
23. Stenton *1948*, 48. On the Lindsey royal genealogy, Stenton *1970*, 129.
24. *Historia Ecclesiae*, chap. 16.
25. This cemetery is unpublished in full: finds in Leicester Mus. Myres *1969*, 76f. for its dating.
26. Hawkes S. *1961* and *1963*.
27. Note, for instance, that one of the Dorchester graves containing such a buckle (Hawkes S. *1961*, 2ff.) is the grave of a woman. Not only a new style of ornament may be involved, but also a new style of para-military dress. Readers in the early 1970s should have no difficulty in believing that this is possible.
28. Coritanian examples are as follows. Leicester: Hawkes S. *1961*, 52 and 63. Osgodby (Lincs.): Lincoln Mus. unpublished. Lincoln: unpublished. Dragonby: unpublished. Saltersford: Hawkes S. *1961*, 57. Kirmington (strap-end): *Lincolnshire Hist. Archaeol.* (1966) fig. 35 & 23. Clipsham: Hawkes S. *1961*, 47.
29. For recent comment, Myres *1969*, 65ff.

30. Unpublished in full: Myres *1952*, 65ff.; *1969*, fig. 26. The urns are in Grantham Mus. and the B.M.
31. Fennell *1964*.
32. Nettleton: *Archaeol. J.* ciii (1946), 89. Fonaby: *Medieval Archaeol.* i (1957), 147f. Meaney *1964*, 155.
33. *Antiq. J.* xxxvi (1956), 189ff.
34. *Trans. Hull Sci. and Field Natur. Club* iv (1918), 311. Finds in Hull Mus.
35. Unpublished.
36. Unpublished, urns in Newark Mus.
37. Webster *1951*, 25ff.
38. *Trans. Thoroton Soc. Nottinghamshire* 1xx (1966), 13ff.
39. Finberg *1955*.

Bibliography

Allen, D.F. (1944) The Belgic dynasties of Britain and their coins, *Archaeologia* xc, 1.

Allen, D.F. (1961) The origins of coinage in Britain, in Frere *1961a*, 97.

Allen, D.F. (1963) *The Coins of the Coritani* (London).

Allen, D.F. (1970) The coins of the Iceni, *Britannia* i, 1.

Allen, D.F. (1971) A Celtic find from a Lincolnshire dyke, in Carson, R.A.G. (ed.), *Mints, Dies and Currency* (London).

Annable, F.K. (1960) *The Romano-British Pottery at Cantley Housing Estate, Doncaster: Kilns 1-8*, Doncaster Mus. Publications no. xxiv.

Applebaum, S. (1958) Agriculture in Roman Britain, *Agr. Hist. Rev.* vi, 66.

Applebaum, S. (1963) The pattern of settlement in Roman Britain, *Agr. Hist. Rev.* xi, 1.

Applebaum, S. (1966) Peasant economy and types of agriculture, in Thomas, A.C. *1966*, 99.

Baker, F.T. (1954) *The Prehistoric Settlement of Lincolnshire*. Unpublished M.A. thesis, Univ. of Nottingham.

Baker, F.T. (1960) The Iron Age salt industry in Lincolnshire, *Rep. Pap. Lincolnshire Archit. Archaeol. Soc.* viii, 26.

Cameron, H. & Lucas, J. (1967) Tripontium, *Trans. Birmingham Archaeol. Soc.* lxxxiii, 130.

Cameron, K. (1959) *The Place-Names of Derbyshire* (Cambridge).

Clark, J.G.D. (1949) Report on excavations on the Cambridgeshire Car Dyke, *Antiq. J.* xxix, 137.

Cleere, H.F. & Bridgewater, N.P. (1966) The iron industry in the Roman period. *Bull.Hist.Metall. Group* vi, 1.

Cockerton, R.W.P. (1960) The Hereward Street, *Derbyshire Archaeol. J.* lxxxi, 71.

Collingwood, R.G. (1937) Roman Britain, in Tenney Frank, *An Economic Survey of Ancient Rome* iii(1937).

Corder, P. (1928) *The Roman Pottery at Crambeck* (York).

Corder, P. (1950) *A Roman-British Pottery Kiln on the Lincoln*

Racecourse (Nottingham).

Corder, P. (1951a) *The Roman Town and Villa at Great Casterton: First Interim Report* (Nottingham).

Corder, P. (1951b) Romano-British buildings and enclosures in Edlington Wood, in Grimes, W.F. *1951*.

Corder, P. (1954a) *The Roman Town and Villa at Great Casterton: Second interim Report* (Nottingham).

Corder, P. (1954b) A Romano-British pottery kiln at Weston Favell, near Northampton, *Antiq. J.* xxxiv, 218.

Corder, P. (1955) The reorganisation of the defences of Romano-British towns in the fourth century, *Archaeol. J.* cii, 20.

Corder, P. (1961) *The Roman Town and Villa at Great Casterton: Third Report* (Nottingham).

Cunliffe, B.W. (1968) *Fifth Report on the Excavations of the Roman Fort at Richborough, Kent, Res. Rep. Soc. Antiq. London,* no. xxiii.

Daniels, C.M. (1966) Excavation of the site of the Roman villa at Southwell, 1959, *Trans. Thoroton Soc. Nottinghamshire* lxx, 13.

Darby, H.C. (1936) *An Historical Geography of England Before A.D.,1800* (Cambridge).

Darby, H.C. (1948) Domesday Woodland in Lincolnshire, *Lincolnshire Hist.* i, 55.

Darby, H.C. (1952) The Lincolnshire wolds, *Lincolnshire Hist.* ix, 315.

Dudley, D.R. & Webster, G. (1965) *The Roman Conquest of Britain* (London).

Dudley, H.E. (1949) *Early Days in North West Lincolnshire* (Scunthorpe).

Ellis, C.D.B. (1969) *History in Leicester* (2nd. ed. Leicester).

Fennell, K.R. (1959) King Street in Kesteven and some notes on Old Sleaford, *Lincolnshire Hist.* ii, 22.

Fennell, K.R. (1964) *The Anglo-Saxon Cemetery at Loveden Hill.* Unpublished Ph.D. thesis, Univ. of Nottingham.

Finberg, H.P.R. (1955) *Roman and Saxon Withington* (Leicester).

Fowler, E. (1968) Hanging bowls, in Coles, J.M. & Simpson, D.D.A. (edd.), *Studies in Ancient Europe* (Leicester).

Fox, C. (1926) *The Archaeology of the Cambridge Region* (Cambridge).

Frere, S.S. (ed.) (1961a) *Problems of the Iron Age in Southern Britain.* Univ. of London Occasional Paper no. xi of the Inst. of Archaeology.

Frere, S.S. (1961b) Some Romano-British sculptures from Ancaster and Wilsford, Lincs., *Antiq. J.* xli, 229.

Frere, S.S. (1967) *Britannia: a History of Roman Britain* (London).

Gillam, J.P. (1939) Romano-British Derbyshire ware, *Derbyshire Archaeol. J.* xix, 429.

Gillam, J.P. (1951) Dales ware, *Antiq. J.* xxxi, 154.

Greenfield, E. (1963) The Romano-British shrines at Brigstock, Northants, *Antiq. J.* xliii, 228.

Greenfield, E. & Webster, G. (1965) Excavations at High Cross, 1955. *Trans. Leicester Archaeol. Soc.* xl, 3.

Grimes, W.F. (1951) *Aspects of Archaeology in Britain and Beyond* (London).

Grimes, W.F. (1961) Some smaller settlements: a symposium, in Frere *1961a*.

Hallam, S.J. (1960) The Romano-British salt industry in South Lincs., *Rep. Pap. Lincolnshire Archit. Archaeol. Soc.* viii, 35.

Hallam, S.J. (1964) Villages in Roman Britain: some evidence, *Antiq. J.* xliv, 19.

Hannah, I.C. (1932) Roman blast furnace in Lincolnshire *Antiq. J.* xii, 262.

Hartley, B.R. (1960) *Notes on the Roman Pottery Industry in the Nene Valley* (Peterborough).

Haseloff, G. (1958) Fragments of a hanging bowl from Bekesbourne, Kent and some ornamental problems, *Medieval Archaeol.* ii, 72

Haverfield, F. (1918) Roman Leicester. *Archaeol. J.* lxxv, 1.

Hawkes, C.F.C. (1945) The Early Iron Age settlement at Fengate, Peterborough. *Archaeol. J.* c, 188.

Hawkes, C.F.C. (1951) Bronze-workers, cauldrons and bucket-animals in Iron Age and Roman Britain, in Grimes *1951*, 172.

Hawkes, S.C. & Dunning, G.C. (1961) Soldiers and settlers in Britain, fourth to fifth century . . . , *Medieval Archaeol.* v, 1.

Hawkes, S.C. (1963) Krieger und Siedler in Britannien während des 4 und 5 Jahrhunderts, *BRGK* xliii-iv, 155.

Hawkes, S.C. (1963) *Some Belgic Brooches from South Ferriby*, Hull Mus. Publications no. 214.

Hobley, B. (1969) A Neronian-Vespasianic military site at 'The Lunt', Baginton, Warwicks. *Trans. Birmingham Archaeol. Soc.* lxxxiii, 65.

Illingworth, C. (1808) *A Topographical Account of the Parish of Scampton* . . .

Jackson, K.H. (1953) *Language and History in Early Britain* (Edinburgh).

Jones, A.H.M. (1964) *The Later Roman Empire* (Oxford).

Jones, G. (1961) Early territorial organization in England and Wales, *Geografiska Annaler* xliii, 174.

Jones, G.D.B. & Webster, P.V. (1969) Derbyshire ware: a reappraisal, *Derbyshire Archaeol. J.* lxxxix, 18.

Kay, S.O. (1956) A Romano-British building in Stubbins Wood, Langwith Jct., near Shirebrook. *Derbyshire Archaeol. J.* lxxvi, 1.

Kendrick, T.D. (1932) British hanging-bowls, *Antiquity* vi, 161.

Kennett, D.H. (1968) The Irchester bowls, *J. Northampton Mus. & Art Gallery* iv, 5.

Kenyon, K.M. (1948) *Excavations at the Jewry Wall Site, Leicester*, *Res. Reps. Soc. Ant. London* no. xv.

Kenyon, K.M. (1950) Excavations at Breedon-on-the-Hill 1946, *Trans. Leicester Archaeol. Soc.* xxvi, 17.

Kilbride-Jones, H.E. (1936) A bronze hanging-bowl from Castle Tioram, Moidart: and a suggested absolute chronology for British hanging-bowls, *Proc. Soc. Antiq. Scotland* lxxi, 206.

King-Fane, W. (1931) The Car Dyke, its origins, object and extent, *Lincolnshire Notes and Queries* xxi, 89.

Lewis, M.J.T. (1966) *Temples in Roman Britain* (Cambridge).

McWhirr, A.D. (1970) The early military history of the Roman East Midlands, *Trans. Leicester Archaeol. Soc.* xlv, 1.

Margary, I.D. (1967) *Roman Roads in Britain* (2nd.ed. London).

Marshall, C.E. (1948) *Guide to the Geology of the East Midlands* (Nottingham).

May, J. (1970) Dragonby: an interim report . . . *Antiq. J.* 1, 222.

May, T. (1922) *The Roman Forts at Templeborough, near Rotherham* (Rotherham).

Meaney, A. (1964) *A Gazetteer of Early Anglo-Saxon Burial Sites* (London).

Mellor, J.E. (1969) Excavations in Leicester 1965-8, *Trans. Leicester Archaeol. Soc.* xliv, 1.

Mertens, J. & Leva, C. (1966) Le fortin de Braives et le 'limes Belgicus', in *Mélanges Piganiol* (Paris).

Morris, J. (1966) Dark Age dates, in Jarrett, M.G. and Dobson, B. (edd.), *Britain and Rome* (Kendal).

Myres, J.N.L. (1951) The Anglo-Saxon pottery of Lincolnshire, *Archaeol. J.* cviii, 65

Myres, J.N.L. (1956) Romano-Saxon pottery, in Harden, D.B. (ed), *Dark Age Britain* (London).

Myres, J.N.L. (1969) *Anglo-Saxon Pottery and the Settlement of England* (Oxford).

Nenquin, J.A.E., (1961) Salt: a study in economic prehistory, *Diss.Arch.Gand.* vi (Bruges).

Oswald, A. (1937a) *The Roman Pottery Kilns at Little London, Torksey* (privately printed).

Oswald, A. (1937b) A Roman fortified villa at Norton Disney, *Antiq. J.* xvii, 138.

Oswald, A. (1949) A re-excavation of the Roman villa at Mansfield Woodhouse (Notts.) 1936-9, *Trans. Thoroton Soc. Nottingham* liii, 1.

Oswald, F. (1927) Margidunum, *Trans. Thoroton Soc. Nottingham* xxxi, 54.

Oswald, F. (1941) Margidunum, *J. Roman Stud.* xxxi, 32.

Oswald, F. (1948) *The Commandant's House at Margidunum* (Nottingham).

Oswald, F. (1952) *Excavation of a Traverse of Margidunum* (Nottingham).

Owen, A.E.B. (1952) Coastal erosion in Eastern Lincolnshire, *Lincolnshire Hist.* ix, 330.

Penny, S.R. (1966) Historical evidence for Roman roads in N.E. Derbyshire, *Derbyshire Archaeol. J.* lxxxvi, 70.

Petch, D.F. (1960) Excavations at Lincoln, 1955-8, *Archaeol. J.* cxvii, 40.

Phillips, C.W. (1933) The present state of archaeology in Lincolnshire: Part I. *Archaeol. J.* xc, 106.

Phillips, C.W. (1934) The present state of archaeology in Lincolnshire: Part II. *Archaeol. J.* xci, 97.

Phillips, C.W. (ed) (1970) *The Fenland in Roman Times*, Royal Geographical Soc., Research Series no. 5 (London)

Pleiner, R. (1964) Die Eisenverhüttung in der 'Germania Magna' zur römischen Kaiserzeit, *BRGK* xlv, 11.

Preston, H. (1917) Romano-British remains at Saltersford, *Lincolnshire Notes and Queries* xiv, 33.

Rahtz, P. (1960) Caistor, *Antiq. J.* xl, 175.

Richmond, I.A. (1946a) The Roman city of Lincoln, *Archaeol. J.* ciii, 26.

Richmond, I.A. (1946b) The four *coloniae* of Roman Britain, *Archaeol. J.* ciii, 37.

Richmond, I.A. (1963a) *Roman Britain* (2nd ed. Harmondsworth).

Richmond, I.A. (1963b) The Cornovii, in Foster, Ll. and Daniel, G. *Culture and Environment* (London), 251.

Richmond, I.A. & Crawford, O.G.S. (1949) The British section of the Ravenna cosmography, *Archaeologia* xciii, 1.

Rivet, A.L.F. (1964) *Town and Country in Roman Britain* (2nd ed. London).

Rivet, A.L.F. (ed.) (1969) *The Roman Villa in Britain* (London).

Rooke, H. (1787) An account of the remains of two Roman villas discovered near Mansfield Woodhouse in May and October 1786, *Archaeologia* viii, 363.

St. Joseph, J.K. (1936) The Roman fort at Brancaster, *Antiq. J.* xvi, 444.

Simpson, M.G. (1964) *Britons and the Roman Army* (London).

Simpson, W.G. (1966) Romano-British settlement on the Welland gravels, in Thomas *1966*, 15.

Smith, J.T. (1963) Romano-British aisled houses, *Archaeol. J.* cxx, 1.

Smith, J.T. (1964) The Roman villa at Denton. *Rep. Pap. Lincolnshire Archit. Archaeol. Soc.* x, 75.

Steers, J.A. (ed.) (1965) *The Cambridge Region* (Cambridge).

Stead, I.M. (1966) Winterton Roman villa: an interim report, *Antiq. J.* xlvi, 72.

Stenton, F.M. (1948) *Anglo-Saxon England* (Oxford).

Stenton, F.M. (1970) *Preparatory to Anglo-Saxon England* (ed. D.M. Stenton) (Oxford).

Swinnerton, H.H. (1931) Post-glacial deposits of the Lincolnshire coast, *Quart J. Geol. Soc.* lxxxvii, 360.

Swinnerton, H.H. (1932) The pottery sites of the Lincolnshire coast, *Antiq. J.* xii, 239.

Swinnerton, H.H. (1938) The physical history of East Lincolnshire. *Trans. Lincolnshire Natur. Union* ix, 91.

Sylvester-Bradley, P.C. & Ford, T.D. (1968) *The Geology of the East Midlands* (Leicester).

Thomas, A.C. (ed.) (1966) *Rural Settlement in Roman Britain*, CBA Res. Rep. VII (London).

Thompson, F.H. (1956) Roman Lincoln, 1953, *J. Roman Stud.* xlvi, 22.

Thompson, F.H. (1958) A Romano-British pottery kiln at N. Hykeham, Lincolnshire: with an Appendix on the typology, dating and distribution of 'Rustic Ware' in Great Britain, *Antiq. J.* xxxviii, 15.

Todd, M. (1966) A large hoard of Early Imperial *aes* from Lincolnshire, *Numis. Chron.* 7 vi, 145.

Todd, M. (1968a) *The Roman Fort at Great Casterton, Rutland* (Nottingham).

Todd, M. (1968b) The commoner Late Roman coarse wares of the East Midlands, *Antiq. J.* xlviii, 192.

Todd, M. (1969) The Roman settlement at Margidunum: the excavations of 1966-8, *Trans. Thoroton Soc. Nottingham* lxxiii, 6.

Todd, M. (1970) The small towns of Roman Britain, *Britannia* i, 114.

Toynbee, J.M.C. (1962) *Art in Roman Britain* (London).

Toynbee, J.M.C. (1964) *Art in Britain under the Romans* (Oxford).

Trollope, E.A. (1870) Ancaster, the Roman *Causennae, Archaeol. J.* xxvii, 1.

Trollope, E.A. (1872) *Sleaford and the Wapentakes of Flaxwell and Aswardhurn* (Sleaford).

Tylecote, R.F. (1962) *Metallurgy in Archaeology* (London).

Tylecote, R.F. (1970) Recent work on early iron-working sites in the Stamford area, *Bull.Hist.Metall. Group* iv, 24.

Walter, J.C. (1908) *A History of Horncastle* (Horncastle).

Walters, H.B. (1910) Romano-British Nottinghamshire, in *VCH Notts*, ii, 1.

Wacher, J.S. (ed.) (1966) *Civitas Capitals of Roman Britain* (Leicester).

Wacher, J.S. (1969) *Excavations at Brough-on-Humber, 1958-61, Res. Reps. Soc. Ant. London*, no. xxv.

Webster, G. (1944) A Roman pottery at South Carlton, Lincs., *Antiq. J.* xxiv, 129.

Webster, G. (1949) The legionary fortress at Lincoln, *J. Roman Stud.* xxxix, 57.

Webster, G. (1951) An Anglo-Saxon Urnfield at South Elkington, Louth, Lincs., *Archaeol. J.* cviii, 25.

Webster, G. (1955) A note on the use of coal in Roman Britain, *Antiq. J.* xxxv, 199.

Webster, G. (1958) The Roman military advance under Ostorius Scapula, *Archaeol J.* cxv, 49.

Webster, G. (1962) Excavations at Rocester, *N. Staffs. J. Field. Stud.* ii, 37.

Webster, G. (1970) The military situations in Britain between A.D. 43 and 71, *Britannia* i, 179.

Webster, G. & Hobley, B. (1964) Aerial reconnaissance over the Warwickshire Avon, *Archaeol. J.* cxxi, 1.

Wheeler, R.E.M. & Wheeler, T.V. (1936) *Verulamium: a Belgic and two Roman Cities, Res. Rep. Soc. Ant. London,* no. xi.

White, D.A. (1961) *Litus Saxonicum* (Madison, Wisconsin).

Whitwell, J.B. (1970) *Roman Lincolnshire* (Lincoln).

Wilson, D.R. (1968) An early Christian cemetery at Ancaster, in Barley, M.W. & Hanson, R.P.C. (edd.), *Christianity in Early Britain, A.D. 300-700* (Leicester) 197.

Woods, P.J. (1969) *Excavations at Hardingstone, Northants, 1967-8,* (Northamptonshire County Council).

Index